Attracting Abundance with EFT*

*Emotional Freedom Techniques

Carol Look, EFT Master
www.AttractingAbundance.com

Crown Media & Printing, Inc.
P.O. Box 3181
Coeur D'Alene, ID 83816-2523
www.crownmediacorp.com

The spirit of this book is dedicated to
some of my favorite people:

Philippa
Frederica
Marieke
Eliza
Jackson

CONTENTS

WELCOME!

I know many of you are traveling on the same path as I am, occasionally enchanted by the exciting gifts that show up along your journey, and sometimes frustrated by the slow progress of manifestations. I am assuming that if you are reading this book, you have been hoping to find ways to create *even more success* in a number of areas in your life. Have you been:

- *Wanting* **more financial abundance?**
- *Searching* **for more spiritual fulfillment?**
- *Looking* **for deeper friendships and love relationships?**
- *Hoping* **for more vibrant health and a stronger body?**
- *Asking* **for unlimited prosperity?**

This book will help you *attract* personal and professional success and live a *prosperous life* full of love, passion, joy and gratitude. There is *plenty* — more than enough for everyone — and you deserve to have all that you want while you enjoy every minute of your life.

You are about to embark on a wonderful journey — using your mind as a *magnet* to *attract more abundance* into your life. In this book you will learn how to use

Emotional Freedom Techniques (EFT) to release all the blocks to financial abundance you may have absorbed, inherited, adopted or picked up since you were born. You will also learn how to use the *Law of Attraction, affirmations, imagery* and *abundance games* to help you reach any other goals you have in mind, such as vibrant health, deeper spiritual connections, fulfilling relationships and anything else on your list.

So...Fasten Your Seatbelts...

HOW BEST TO USE THIS BOOK

This book is divided into a short section outlining **EFT** directions, followed by four parts corresponding to the "**4 Steps to Attracting Abundance**." At the end of each of these sections, I outline two *Abundance Games* that I have used personally to attract abundance with great success. Based on the results I have had, I highly recommend these "games."

There are of course several options for how best to use this book. Choose from the list of options below, based on whatever you *want* to do, or what *pulls* you (not what you think you *should* do).

Read from start to finish, noting which sections will be most relevant for your *personal* issues. Return to relevant sections.

or

Read through the <u>Table of Contents</u> and choose which *Steps* you need to work on. Start with the Step that most "speaks" to you.

or

Read a few pages a day and work through the book at a steady yet leisurely pace.

or

Randomly choose pages for study and follow the *Abundance Games* and EFT suggestions in this fashion.

or

Let your intuition guide you! Trust where your inner guidance takes you...

WHAT IS ABUNDANCE ANYWAY?

**Webster's Dictionary** defines _**ABUNDANCE**_ as follows:

— _**great plenty; an overflowing quantity; ample sufficiency; fullness, overflowing;**_

— Commonly used synonyms are _**plenteousness, exuberance, plenty, riches, affluence, copiousness, wealth.**_

Usually, my clients desire more _**financial abundance**_ in their lives. However, since resistance to receiving any of your desires is caused by the same energetic _**vibration**_, this book will cover _**all**_ areas in which you want more success. While the primary focus of the **EFT** exercises will be on increasing your _**financial abundance**_, you will be able to use the **EFT** exercises for improving relationships, increasing vibrant health, attracting professional opportunities, and deepening spiritual connections by _**raising your energetic vibration**_.

Whenever I feel a lack of financial abundance, I remember how many loving friends I have, how many incredible coincidences have occurred in my life, and how many times I have felt deeply blessed. Sometimes I focus on how many wonderful books I've read or the many glorious vacations I've enjoyed. I do this just to trigger the feeling of *abundance*. Reminding myself of the *abundance* in my life helps me get back on track for *financial prosperity* in a hurry, because the truth is, no matter what's in my bank account, I have lived a life full of incredible bliss and blessings.

After reading this exciting book, I expect that you will feel convinced that you are able to attract *more than enough* (that is, *abundance*) in *every* area of your life. I will lead you through dozens of **EFT** exercises as well as other useful, fun techniques and games to address the **4 - step process** I use in seminars, individual sessions, and in my audio CD series.

THE

4 STEPS

TO

INCREASE

ABUNDANCE

THE 4 STEPS
TO INCREASE ABUNDANCE

#1. Clear Blocks to Success and Abundance

#2. Increase Your Prosperity Consciousness

#3. Activate the Law of Attraction

#4. Claim Abundance NOW

EVERYTHING

IS

ABOUT

VIBRATION

EVERYTHING IS ABOUT *VIBRATION*

Before we start applying **EFT** to these 4 steps, I want to talk to you about *VIBRATION,* or basically, what makes the world go 'round. Everything holds its own *vibration* — colors, words, people, places, foods, attitudes — and when you can learn to change your *vibration* so that it *attracts the abundance* that you want rather than repels it, your life will change immediately. *We are always vibrating*, so it makes sense to control these *vibrational states* for our advantage. The easiest way to raise your personal *vibration* in order to *attract* what you want is by using **EFT** to address the above-mentioned 4 steps. Consider these questions:

- When you think about *money*, what is your *vibration* about it?

- When you think of your *body*, how are you *vibrating*?

- What about when you think of finding a *perfect life partner*? What feelings surface?

If anything other than joy or relaxation surfaces when you focus on these topics, you are not *vibrating* in a place that will *pull* what you want towards you.

My mother finds it soothing to collect and read cookbooks. And she knows when she *follows the recipe* for a chicken dish, that's what she will get! It's guaranteed. She doesn't expect to get lasagna when she uses chicken and onions.

The same is true for *abundance* and *manifestation*. There are specific *recipes*. You will take out of the oven (*manifest*) whatever you put into the pot (*vibrate, intend, ask for*). It's really quite simple. Unfortunately, people (myself included) just refuse to *follow the recipe* exactly. We always want to add other ingredients, and in this case, usually ingredients that slow down the cooking process. Ask any chef in the world and they will agree: *RECIPES WORK!* But you need to follow them.

FOCUS,

CHOICE

&

LAW

OF

ATTRACTION

FOCUS, CHOICE
&
LAW OF ATTRACTION

I love the notion of *choice*. When I have *choices*, I feel *free*. When I am *free*, I feel better. When I feel better, I am more relaxed. When I am more relaxed and *free*, I am automatically *vibrating* in a better place and I find that what I want is naturally drawn towards me, *with very little effort*. Honestly, it feels as if I am cheating, and that this is too good to be true. Try it, and you'll see what I mean.

What I expect this book will do for you is help you decide where and what to focus on and how to *control your mind* so you *attract* or bring more of whatever you want into your life. Your *focus is your choice*; no one else is responsible for making you have a bad day.

As I mentioned before, **EFT** is the best and easiest tool to help us clean up our focus and *vibrate* on a joyful plane, which will in turn *magnetize* our desires right into our lives. We live and operate in a world of *magnetic attraction*; we just don't make the most efficient use of it.

Did I say *magnetic attraction*??? Yes! Our thoughts cause a *vibration* and our *vibration* emits a signal, and anything similar to that signal is drawn *as if by a magnet*, to us. This is called the *Law of Attraction* and you could be using it every day to help you realize your wildest dreams.

Actually, you *are* using it every day, but you probably aren't aware of how powerful it is or how much influence it has on your life. While I have read dozens of authors regarding the *Law of Attraction* (see my *recommended reading list*) my favorite source of information and explanation of the *Law of Attraction* can be found through **www.abraham-hicks.com**. Combining **EFT** with the Abraham-Hicks material made the difference in my life between being financially comfortable and being *incredibly abundant*.

EFT will help you *activate* the *Law of Attraction* and point you in the right direction. You will no longer inadvertently use this law as a way to sabotage yourself or rob yourself of joy. *RECIPES WORK...* but you need to follow them.

BELIEFS

&

EXPECTATIONS

BELIEFS & EXPECTATIONS

Did you know that the *beliefs* you hold consciously or in your subconscious mind *are compulsive*? What this means is that whatever you *believe* in your subconscious mind must come true, *no matter what*. If you believe you are not good enough, or that you do not deserve financial success, you will move heaven and earth to achieve this outcome. Similarly, if you believe success comes naturally to you, you will in fact *attract success* easily into your life.

Since there is no way to change the fact that our brains deal with our beliefs compulsively — *we will always fulfill our beliefs no matter what* — the next best thing is to *change our beliefs and expectations* so we end up at the right destination. How do we accomplish this? With **EFT**, of course! **EFT** is the premier tool to help you *change your beliefs and expectations* so that what you desire comes naturally to you, without all the pushing and struggling.

Yes, I too was taught that to make more money I had to work harder and keep up the struggle, and by all means, suffer. I could have fun on the side, but only at the expense of my savings account. I have since learned, thanks to some wonderful teachings, new and old, that it is not your struggle that makes you wealthy, but your *vibration* about whatever you do. It doesn't matter if you are a therapist, an artist, a conductor or a janitor.

There's that strange word again, *vibration*. Remember, if you control your *vibration*, you can control what you *attract* into your life on every level...health, wealth and love, just to name a few. If you believe in lack or expect you will always encounter scarcity, you will receive lack and scarcity consistently. If you honestly **believe in abundance**, you will be shocked at how quickly your desires are *manifested.* If you find yourself annoyed at this simple equation, try it for 30 days before you make any decisions about whether it works or not. While it may seem like just a theory to you now, when you use the techniques presented in this book and see the results, you will *have* and *be* living proof that *vibrations* make all the difference in the world. You are like a television set that has been left *ON* 24 hours a day—you are *vibrating* all day long. Why not choose the channels you want?

I will be demonstrating how to use **EFT** to improve and raise your *vibration* by changing your emotions whenever you wish on an hourly, weekly and monthly basis. When you delete negative beliefs and **raise your vibration**, you **attract** more of your desires in your life. Some of the emotions that will help you **attract** more of what you want are:

- joy
- delight
- gratitude

- appreciation
- love
- passion
- bliss
- ecstasy

When you focus on these feelings, you are inevitably *raising your vibration* to a higher level, and thus speeding up the *magnetization* (or *attraction*) of your financial or personal goals. Some of the feelings that are a natural drag on your *vibration*, slowing down the realization of your goals, are:

- fear
- helplessness
- resentment/ anger
- hatred
- jealousy
- envy
- irritation
- shame

Since we are human, we all have the capacity to feel every one of these emotions. The point is *not* to pretend you don't feel negative emotions. The point is to *notice* when you do, *decide* if you want to do something about it, and *choose* one of the wonderful tools I offer in this book to change your feeling, redirect your focus, and *raise your vibration* when you wish to.

DISCLAIMER

The information presented in this book is educational in nature and is provided only as general information. As part of the information presented in this book, you will be introduced to a healing modality called Emotional Freedom Techniques ("EFT") which is a technique referred to as a type of energy therapy. Due to the experimental nature of EFT, and because it is a relatively new healing approach and the extent of its effectiveness, as well as its risks and benefits have not been fully researched, you agree to assume and accept full responsibility for any and all risks associated with using EFT as a result of reading this book. You agree and understand that the information contained in this book is only for your personal use. You further understand that if you choose to use EFT, it is possible that emotional or physical sensations or additional unresolved memories may surface which could be perceived as negative side effects.

The information presented in this book is not intended to represent that EFT is used to diagnose, treat, cure, or prevent any disease or psychological disorder. EFT is not a substitute for medical or psychological/mental health treatment. Any stories or testimonials presented in this book do not constitute a warranty, guarantee, or prediction regarding the outcome of an individual using EFT for any particular issue. Further, you understand that the author makes no warranty, guarantee, or prediction regarding any outcome for you using EFT for any particular issue. While all materials and references to other resources are given in good faith, the accuracy, validity, effectiveness, completeness, or usefulness of any information in this book, cannot be guaranteed. The author accepts no responsibility or liability whatsoever for the use or misuse of the information contained in this book, including links to other resources. The author strongly advises that you seek professional advice as appropriate before making any health decision.

EMOTIONAL

FREEDOM

TECHNIQUES

(EFT)

EFT

EFT is a form of psychological acupuncture that uses light tapping with your fingertips instead of inserting needles to stimulate traditional Chinese acupuncture points. The *tapping* on these designated points on the face and body is combined with verbalizing the *identified problem* (or *target*) followed by a *general affirmation phrase*. Combining these ingredients of the **EFT** technique *balances the energy system* and appears to relieve psychological stress and physiological pain. Restoring the balance of the energy system allows the body and mind to resume their natural healing abilities. **EFT** is safe, easy to apply, and is non-invasive.

HOW YOU WILL USE EFT
TO ATTRACT ABUNDANCE

Over the years, I have developed dozens of **EFT** tapping exercises for *attracting abundance*, and I am presenting them together here for the first time in print. The **EFT** exercises are designed to target the specific blocks you may have to *receiving abundance* in your life. Whether you are searching for an increase in financial wealth, more vibrant health or deeper and more fulfilling relationships, **EFT** and the ***Abundance Games*** will help you reach your goals.

Here is how you will perform the exercises. Each **EFT** tapping exercise will consist of a **SETUP STATEMENT**, followed by two **ROUNDS** of tapping the sequence of **8 EFT** points. **ROUND #1 focuses on the problem** by repeating the ***negative reminder phrase*** while **ROUND #2 focuses on the solution** by verbalizing preferences, choices, and possible alternative outcomes.

EFT DIRECTIONS

SETUP STATEMENT:

- **Choose a target for EFT** --- an emotion, a block, a belief, or an abundance issue.

- **Scale the intensity of the feeling, belief or abundance issue being addressed on the Intensity Scale of 0-10** (where 0=no discomfort and 10=strong discomfort), or just make a note of how you feel.

- **Tap the karate chop point** (see diagram) on either one of your hands continuously while repeating the entire **SETUP STATEMENT** listed for each abundance issue. (The **SETUP STATEMENT** combines the **target** and an **affirmation**. An example of a **SETUP STATEMENT** might be *"Even though I have these money blocks, I deeply and completely accept myself."*)

NEGATIVE TAPPING SEQUENCE:

- **Starting at the eyebrow point,** begin tapping each point in the sequence of 8 points (see below) approximately 7 - 10 times while repeating the *negative reminder phrase* provided for each issue.

SEQUENCE OF TAPPING POINTS:

- **Eyebrow**
- **Side of Eye**
- **Under Eye**
- **Under Nose**
- **Chin**
- **Collarbone**
- **Under Arm**
- **Top of Head**

This directs your mind to focus on the negative thought patterns that block your ability to attract abundance and **allows EFT to neutralize them.**

POSITIVE TAPPING SEQUENCE:

- **There are 8 positive phrases provided for each abundance issue.**

- **Starting at the eyebrow point again,** tap each point approximately 7-10 times while repeating a different phrase for each of the 8 tapping points indicated.

- **This allows you to install what you would *prefer* to experience emotionally in your thought patterns and in your life.**

DEEP BREATH:

- **Complete each exercise with a slow deep breath to help move the energy through your body.**

EFT TAPPING POINTS

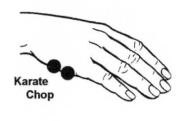

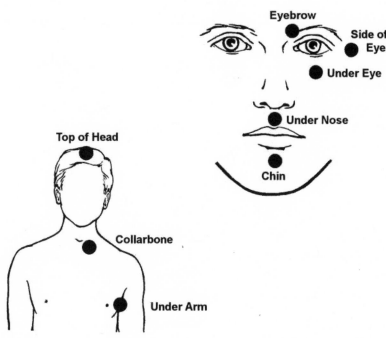

THE 0-10 POINT INTENSITY SCALE

The **Intensity Scale** is a scale of measurement from 0-10, where 0= no discomfort at all, and 10= an incredibly high rating of emotional discomfort about the issue you have identified (targeted) to work on with **EFT**.

You can also measure the "truth" of a limiting belief or expectation with this scale. **EFT** practitioners take the measurement before and after completing one or more rounds of **EFT**. You could also call the scale of measurement the "Upset Chart" or the "Truth Meter." It doesn't matter what you call it, the point is that using the **Intensity Scale** helps you track your progress when doing **EFT**.

The reason it is important to track your progress is that oftentimes it is easy to "forget" how terrible the original problem felt to you, and you may not give much weight to your newfound relief after using **EFT**. It can be difficult to *notice the absence* of something unpleasant, and using the **Intensity Scale** will help you see the "before and after" results. Also, using the **Intensity Scale** helps you identify which pieces or players in your "story" you need to work on – just mention them out loud and measure the intensity from 0-10.

Not everyone uses the 0-10 point **Intensity Scale** when doing **EFT**. However, it's a great way to measure your progress so you can decide whether to move on to a new issue or whether you need to tap more on your original feeling or event you targeted.

The **Intensity Scale** can be used to measure a variety of responses:

- *How true* does the belief feel from 0-10?
- *How intense* is your discomfort from 0-10?
- *How true* does this *statement* feel to you on the 0-10 point scale?
- *How upset* do you feel about this?
- *How much* do you want this?
- *How anxious* are you?

Using the 0-10 point scale before starting a round of **EFT** will let you know *how much this issue or past event truly bothers you now*. I always ask my clients to measure their number on the scale from their gut feeling, not from an intellectual perspective. Sometimes people will answer, *"Well I know I shouldn't feel this way because we all deserve success..."* However, it's important to be clear: I want to hear how high or low the actual *feeling* and *rating* is on the scale, not the "should" or "shouldn't."

So we take a measurement before and after each round of **EFT**. This will tell us the following information:

- Are you tuned into the issue?
- Are you noticing emotional improvement?
- Are you getting distracted by other aspects of the problem?
- Is the *SETUP STATEMENT* on target for you?

So, for example, suppose you don't believe you deserve success of any kind. I would ask you to (1) repeat the sentence out loud, and then (2) measure the "truth" of it on the 0-10 point **Intensity Scale**.

- *I don't believe I deserve success* _____ (0-10)

After tapping for a few rounds on *"I don't believe I deserve success"* measure **how true** this statement feels to you now. It is highly likely the "truth" of this statement will have dropped on the measurement scale. However, what is more important is to identify whether any specific events have surfaced for you that **support this belief**. Some possibilities are below:

- The time my coach said I didn't deserve to be on the team…
- The time my father said I didn't deserve to be successful…
- The time the teacher said I didn't deserve success…

Take each of these specific events and measure the intensity of the *emotional charge* when you think about them. This will give you more specific targets for **EFT**. Measure before and after your tapping.

SPECIFIC EVENTS

When using **EFT**, identifying and collapsing the *emotional charge* you feel from past, specific events that are contributing to your current concerns will greatly enhance your overall success. Our current feeling states, moods and levels of stress are formed by emotional responses and subsequent chemical reactions to specific events in our lives.

These events and chemical reactions are *stored* in our cellular, physical and emotional memories, and when something in the present day looks or feels similar to the old event, *we react again as if we have encountered the original event*.

When someone tells me **EFT** isn't working on them, I immediately suspect that their **EFT** statements have been too global and too general to collapse the negative charge they feel in their mind and body about whichever target they have chosen.

For example, when someone tells me they have been tapping on "low self-esteem" I know they will not be progressing very far with **EFT**. While the person may indeed have low self-esteem, the topic is too general a target for **EFT** to yield satisfactory results.

If you want to work on what you refer to as your low self-esteem, it would be helpful to break this issue down into smaller, more specific bits of information. For instance:

- How do you know you have low self-esteem?
- Who taught you that you weren't worthy?
- What did he/she say to you to make you think you weren't deserving?
- When was the first time you heard or believed you didn't measure up?
- What exactly did "they" say to you?
- What specific event can you remember that taught you about your worth?

The answers to all of these questions will provide more specific, emotionally-laden targets for your **EFT** tapping exercises to clear your low self-esteem.

Other themes and questions that may help you to identify specific events that have contributed to some of your limiting beliefs about attracting success and abundance are as follows:

- **Safety**
  - Why don't you feel safe becoming more successful?
  - What feels safe about staying where you are?

- **Identity**
  - Who will you be if you change?
  - How will they react to you if you change?

- **Fear of Change**
  - What else might happen in your life?
  - What happened the last time you changed?

- **Fear of Success**
  - What are you afraid of?
  - Why is success not safe for you?

- **What is the *downside* of getting what you want?**

- **What is the *upside* of staying exactly where you are?**

- **If you could do it again...**
  - Who would you like to omit from your life?
  - What events stand out in your memory the most?
  - When were you the most unhappy, the most scared?

HOW TO FIND YOUR EFT TARGET

Getting more specific by identifying the best **target** for **EFT** will help you make more significant progress when using **EFT** to clear the emotional issues that are blocking your abundance. Try answering the questions and filling in the blanks below:

- The subject of the story with the most emotion:

  - When you think of your childhood or more recent times, what subject matter has the most "charge" on it for you? This will be the *target* for your tapping.
  - When you think of high school, which friend or classmate triggers the most intensity in your gut?
  - When you think of your family, who stands out as the one who scared you? Betrayed you? Misunderstood you?

- When you say particular words, which ones give you what feels like an *electrical charge* in your body? These will be the **targets** for your tapping. For example, repeat these words and measure the "charge" on them:

- School
- Playmates
- Dinnertime
- Loneliness
- Nighttime
- Homework
- Breakup
- Anger
- Resentment
- Unfair

- Fill in the blanks:

  - My least favorite emotion is _____.
  - My least favorite family member is _____.
  - My worst memory from grade school is _____.
  - My worst memory from high school is _____.
  - The person who hurt me the most is _____.
  - The person I trust the least is _____.
  - The person who betrayed me the most was _____.
  - The family member who never understood me is _____.
  - The time I experienced the most injustice was _____.

The words, names and feelings you filled in to these blanks will lead you to effective tapping targets with **EFT**.

TELL THE STORY

EFT founder Gary Craig devised some wonderful techniques to help those of us using **EFT** to identify specific events without flooding ourselves with too many uncomfortable emotions. One of my favorite techniques is the *Tell The Story Technique*.

Choose a story that gives you a significant "charge" on the 0-10 point **Intensity Scale**. Tell the story out loud to yourself, a friend or counselor, and *tap continuously while you tell the story*. There's no need to stop and devise **SETUP STATEMENTS**, no need to check numbers or choose targets, *just tell the story and tap while you tell it*. (You may need to do this several times before noticing that thinking about the original story and telling it out loud doesn't create any discomfort.)

As you tell your story, you will notice that certain parts or scenes from the story will feel more emotionally charged than others at different times. As you collapse one "aspect" after another, you will be able to tell the entire story, start to finish, without any emotional discomfort.

SAMPLE EFT EXERCISE

This **sample EFT exercise** will lead you through a typical **EFT treatment round.** It includes **the following steps:**

(1) CHOOSE A TARGET

(2) RATE THE INTENSITY ON THE 0-10 POINT SCALE

(3) REPEAT THE SETUP STATEMENT (3 times)

(4) PERFORM THE NEGATIVE TAPPING ROUND

(5) PERFORM THE POSITIVE TAPPING ROUND

Repeat out loud, *"I feel anxious about all my expenses."* On the 0-10 point **Intensity Scale**, how true does this feel?

*(While tapping on your **karate chop point** on either hand, repeat the following **Setup Statement 3 times.**)*

> *Even though **I feel anxious about all my expenses**, I deeply and completely accept myself.*

Now tap the sequence of points while repeating the **NEGATIVE REMINDER PHRASE**, *"I feel anxious about all my expenses."*

ROUND #1: Negative Reminder Phrase

*(Repeat the following **reminder phrase** while tapping the sequence of 8 tapping points.)*

> *I feel anxious about all my expenses.*

Now that you have completed one full round of EFT, repeat the phrase out loud again: *"I feel anxious about all my expenses"* and measure *how true* it feels NOW (after one round of tapping) on the 0-10 point **Intensity Scale**. Hopefully, the level of anxiety about the topic of money will have decreased. If not, continue with one or two more "negative" rounds until your **Intensity Scale** rating has dropped.

Then perform ROUND #2 *with positive words reflecting your desired outcome.* Repeat a different phrase for each of the 8 tapping points indicated, from the **eyebrow** to the **top of the head.**

ROUND #2: Positive Phrases

(Repeat a different phrase for each of the 8 tapping points.)

(eyebrow) I love knowing I can feel calm about money...

(side of eye) I choose to feel relaxed even though I have these expenses...

(under eye) It feels so right to be free of this anxiety...

(under nose) I appreciate how much I have changed...

(chin) I love knowing I resolved this conflict...

(collarbone) I choose to release this anxiety now...

(under arm) It feels so right to be calm about my expenses...

(head) I love appreciating what I have.

STEP #1

CLEAR BLOCKS

TO

SUCCESS

&

ABUNDANCE

STEP #1
CLEAR BLOCKS TO
SUCCESS & ABUNDANCE

The most important question regarding any blocks to abundance is:

- **What *limiting beliefs* and *emotional conflicts* are keeping you from being successful?**

You may indeed *want* more ***financial abundance***, but if you have internal conflicts that cause you to struggle to reach your goals, you will forever be waiting for success in your life. If you answer **YES** to any of the questions in this section, you probably have some ***unconscious (or conscious) blocks*** to success:

- **Do you ever find that you sabotage yourself *just as* you become aware of your increasing success?**

This is a classic sign that you have ***unconscious blocks*** to being successful in some area of your life. Many clients tell me ***they just can't help themselves***. They feel compelled to do something foolish that inhibits their success. They procrastinate, they show up late, or forget something important for a successful outcome of a job. All of these behaviors, of course, sabotage their progress.

In the following **EFT Setup Statements** and **EFT Rounds**, remember:

- **Repeat the Setup Statement three times out loud.**

- **Tap the sequence of points while saying the highlighted phrases.**

- **Move to the positive round and tap the points again.**

ISSUE: PROCRASTINATION BLOCKS MY ABUNDANCE

Engaging in the common habit of procrastination is an easy way to block abundance. Ask yourself the following questions:

- What's the **UPSIDE** to my procrastination?
- What's in it for me?
- What's the **payoff** for procrastinating?
- Assuming my procrastinating is a **solution** to something…what conflict does it solve?
- Does it keep me **safe** from criticism?
- Does it keep me **protected** from being judged?
- Does it give me a way to **rebel**?

If you could view your procrastination as *an attempt at finding a solution to an emotional conflict*, you will easily detect the real reason you procrastinate.

Maybe you're acting out your anger/resentment at an authority figure, or maybe you view procrastination as a legitimate way to rebel against rules.

Repeat the phrases below out loud and measure how true they feel on the 0-10 point **Intensity Scale**:

- *I procrastinate to protect myself from being judged and criticized* _____ (0-10)

- ***I'm afraid of being judged and criticized***
  _____ (0-10)

If you can think of a specific event these phrases remind you of, make a note of it and use it as a target for **EFT** at a later date.

*(Repeat the following **setup statement** 3 times while tapping the **karate chop point**.)*

> *Even though **I procrastinate to protect myself from being judged and criticized**, I deeply and completely love and accept who I am.*

ROUND #1: Negative Reminder Phrase

*(Repeat the following **reminder phrase** while tapping the sequence of 8 tapping points.)*

> ***I procrastinate to protect myself from being judged and criticized.***

ROUND #2: Positive Phrases

(Repeat a different phrase for each of the 8 tapping points.)

(eyebrow) I choose to feel safe even if I complete my projects...

(side of eye) I know I am safe even though they may judge me...

(under eye) I choose to move forward and feel safe...

(under nose) I no longer need to procrastinate...

(chin) I choose to move forward steadily and safely...

(collarbone) I appreciate who I am...

(under arm) I choose to appreciate who I am...

(head) I'm so relieved I no longer need to procrastinate.

Repeat the phrases below again out loud and measure how true they feel now on the 0-10 point **Intensity Scale**:

- *I procrastinate to protect myself from being judged and criticized* _____ (0-10)

- *I'm afraid to be judged or criticized* _____ (0-10)

You may wish to continue tapping on this fear that supports your procrastinating behavior, or move on to the next **EFT** target.

ISSUE: FEAR OF SUCCESS

Say out loud: *I'm afraid to become too successful...* How true does this feel on the 0-10 point **Intensity Scale**?

*(Repeat the following **setup statement** 3 times while tapping the **karate chop point**.)*

---

*Even though **I'm afraid to become too successful**, I deeply and completely accept and love all of me.*

ROUND #1: Negative Reminder Phrase

*(Repeat the following **reminder phrase** while tapping the sequence of 8 tapping points.)*

I'm afraid to become too successful.

Before beginning the positive round, measure the "truth" of this statement again on the 0-10 point **Intensity Scale**.

- *I'm afraid to become too successful* _____ (0-10)

If the intensity number hasn't dropped significantly, continue tapping for the fear, or identify reasons "why" you are afraid to become successful, and use those reasons as your next targets for **EFT**.

ROUND #2: Positive Phrases

(Repeat a different phrase for each of the 8 tapping points.)

(eyebrow) I can feel safe becoming successful...

(side of eye) I appreciate the success I have...

(under eye) I enjoy abundance...

(nose) I choose to feel safe and successful now...

(chin) I feel confident about becoming successful...

(collarbone) I appreciate the success I already enjoy...

(under arm) I enjoy abundance and plenty...

(head) I choose to feel safe and successful now.

ISSUE: SABOTAGE

Repeat the phrases below out loud and measure *how true* they feel in your gut on the 0-10 point **Intensity Scale**:

- *I can't stop sabotaging myself* ____ (0-10)

- *I feel frustrated with my sabotaging* ____ (0-10)

*(Repeat the following **setup statement** 3 times while tapping the **karate chop point**.)*

---

*Even though **I can't stop sabotaging myself**, I deeply and completely love and accept myself anyway.*

ROUND #1: Negative Reminder Phrase

*(Repeat the following **reminder phrase** while tapping the sequence of 8 tapping points.)*

I keep sabotaging myself.

ROUND #2: Positive Phrases

(Repeat a different phrase for each of the 8 tapping points.)

(eyebrow) I choose to accept how successful I am...

(side of eye) I'm releasing my need to sabotage myself...

(under eye) I love feeling free of those old patterns...

(under nose) I choose to embrace my success now...

(chin) I choose to accept how successful I am...

(collarbone) I'm happy I've released my sabotage habit...

(under arm) I love feeling free of sabotage...

(head) I choose to own my success now.

ISSUE: I'D RATHER FEEL SAFE THAN SUCCESSFUL

- What do you mean by this statement?
- Does being successful feel unsafe to you?
- What might happen to you if you are successful?
- Are you willing to sacrifice being successful in order to feel safe?
- Do you feel safe now because you're not successful?

If you don't feel safe with success, you will compulsively sabotage your efforts at getting what you want. *Safety is of primary importance to us as human beings. Having money, love, peace of mind or material goods pales in comparison to feeling safe on an energetic level.*

I recommend identifying *why you wouldn't feel safe* if you become very successful. Again, the most important question may be, *"What happened the last time you were successful?"* If there are specific events that you associate with the last time you were successful, they should become targets for **EFT**.

Measure the "truth" of these statements:

- *I don't feel safe being successful* _____ (0-10)

- *I have a conflict about being successful* __ (0-10)

- *I'd rather be safe than successful* _____ (0-10)

*(Repeat the following **setup statements** while tapping the **karate chop point**.)*

*Even though **I don't feel safe being successful**, I deeply and profoundly love and accept myself anyway... Even though **getting what I want doesn't feel safe to me**, I choose to accept that I have this conflict... Even though **I have a conflict about becoming successful**, I accept who I am and how I feel.*

ROUND #1: Negative Reminder Phrase

*(Repeat the following **reminder phrase** while tapping the sequence of 8 tapping points.)*

I'd rather feel safe than successful.

Before proceeding to **Round #2**, measure the "truth" of the following statement again, and notice whether the emotional charge on it has been reduced, or whether there are any specific events that contribute to this fear.

- *I'd rather feel safe than successful* _____ (0-10)

ROUND #2: Positive Phrases

(Repeat a different phrase for each of the 8 tapping points.)

(eyebrow) I choose to find new ways to feel safe and successful...

(side of eye) I know I can feel safe even if I'm successful...

(under eye) I can erase those old programs right now...

(under nose) I deserve to be successful...

(chin) I choose to feel safe and successful...

(collarbone) I am as safe as I choose to be...

(under arm) I choose to accept my feelings and move on...

(head) I feel confident and joyful about my success.

ISSUE: BLOCKING SUCCESS

*(Repeat the following **setup statement** 3 times while tapping the **karate chop point**.)*

> Even though **I can't get out of my own way**, I choose to release this conflict.

ROUND #1: Negative Reminder Phrase

*(Repeat the following **reminder phrase** while tapping the sequence of 8 tapping points.)*

> *I can't get out of my own way.*

ROUND #2: Positive Phrases

(Repeat a different phrase for each of the 8 tapping points.)

(eyebrow) I love knowing I resolved this conflict...

(side of eye) I have successfully gotten out of my own way...

(under eye) I love being successful...

(under nose) I intend to embrace the success that is mine...

(chin) I successfully resolved this conflict...

(collarbone) I finally got out of my own way...

(under arm) I love being successful...

(head) I intend to embrace all the success I deserve.

ISSUE: IF I GET WHAT I WANT, I COULD LOSE IT

This statement rings true for so many people! They actually sabotage getting what they want, for fear that their success heightens the risk of losing and *being without* what they want. When they didn't have "it" they weren't in any danger! This pattern goes for money, relationships, opportunities and material objects.

You can't lose something you don't have and this is frequently used as a legitimate excuse by millions of people to actually avoid relationships, professional risks, opportunities and experimenting with new ideas.

- Is this fear holding you back?
- Is there another time in your life when you got what you wanted and lost it? (This would be a good specific event as a **target** for **EFT**.)
- When was something valuable taken from you?
- Test the following statements on the 0-10 point **Intensity Scale**:
    - **I'm afraid I'll lose it once I get it** _____ **(0-10)**
    - **I'm afraid it will happen again** _____ **(0-10)**
    - **It's not worth the risk** _____ **(0-10)**
    - **I'd rather not be vulnerable to losing it** _____ **(0-10)**

People are often unaware that they have this conflict about reaching their goals, and spend way too much time alternating between moving forward, sabotaging, moving forward and sabotaging again.

*(Repeat the following **setup statements** while tapping the **karate chop point**.)*

> *Even though **I'm afraid if I get what I want I will lose it**, I deeply and profoundly love and accept myself anyway...Even though **it's not worth the risk**, and I'd rather stay safe, I accept who I am right now...Even though **I have this conflict about manifesting my desires**, I deeply and profoundly love and accept myself anyway.*

ROUND #1: Negative Reminder Phrase

*(Repeat the following **reminder phrase** while tapping the sequence of 8 tapping points.)*

> ***I'm afraid if I get what I want I might lose it.***

Before proceeding to the positive round of solutions, measure the "truth" of this statement again:

- ***I'm afraid if I get what I want I might lose it***
  _____ (0-10)

Perform a few more rounds of **EFT** using the original *Setup Statement* (*Even though I'm afraid if I get what I want I might lose it...*) until the "truth" of this statement is reduced significantly. Then proceed to the positive phrases below.

ROUND #2: Positive Phrases

(Repeat a different phrase for each of the 8 tapping points.)

(eyebrow) I choose to feel calm and confident...

(side of eye) I choose to accept and take this risk...

(under eye) I choose to appreciate this conflict about success...

(under nose) I deserve to enjoy what I manifest...

(chin) I choose to accept myself in spite of this conflict...

(collarbone) I choose to appreciate the depth of this conflict...

(under arm) I choose to appreciate who I am anyway...

(head) I feel calm and confident about taking the risk.

ISSUE: I MAKE MYSELF FAIL

*(Repeat the following **setup statement** 3 times while tapping the **karate chop point**.)*

> *Even though **I don't know why I make myself fail**, I choose to accept all of my conflicts.*

ROUND #1: Negative Reminder Phrase

*(Repeat the following **reminder phrase** while tapping the sequence of 8 tapping points.)*

> *I don't know why I make myself fail.*

ROUND #2: Positive Phrases

(Repeat a different phrase for each of the 8 tapping points.)

(eyebrow) I have released the need to sabotage…

(side of eye) I love knowing I am clear now…

(under eye) I love receiving the guidance from within…

(under nose) I appreciate that I have changed…

(chin) Now I want to be successful…

(collarbone) I love knowing I am clear about success…

(under arm) I love receiving the guidance from within…

(head) I appreciate that I have changed.

- **Do you ever find yourself feeling guilty because you have more than others?**

"Sara" feels guilty because she has a higher paying job than her peers, and often has to "pretend" she doesn't have enough money to dine out or buy new clothes. Sara is typical of many of my clients who were told they were lucky to have what they already had and *shouldn't want* anything more. When these people have normal, healthy desires, they feel guilty. Guilt never makes other people have more, and never attracts abundance into your life.

- **Are you afraid of becoming wealthy because of other people's reactions?**

Many of my clients have been on the receiving end of envy and jealousy from peers or family members. As a result, they sabotage themselves so they can avoid being the recipient of this often hostile behavior.

- **Do you see wealthy people as greedy, lucky, mean or unfair?**

If you view rich people as greedy or unfair, do you see why you would block your own wealth? Why would you want to become someone who is greedy or mean? This is a common but simple emotional block that can be efficiently neutralized with **EFT**.

The themes of guilt, fear of other people's reactions and negative views of wealthy people will be addressed in the following **EFT** tapping exercises...

ISSUE: GUILT ABOUT HAVING MORE

Repeat the following phrase and measure how high your guilt feels on the 0-10 point **Intensity Scale**:

- *I feel guilty because I have more than others*
  _____ (0-10)

*(Repeat the following **setup statement** 3 times while tapping the **karate chop point**.)*

> *Even though **I feel guilty because I have more than others**, I choose to feel good about myself.*

ROUND #1: Negative Reminder Phrase

*(Repeat the following **reminder phrase** while tapping the sequence of 8 tapping points.)*

> *I feel guilty because I have more than others.*

Before proceeding to the positive phrases, measure the level of guilt again and notice whether it has decreased or not.

- *I feel guilty because I have more than others*
  _____ (0-10)

ROUND #2: Positive Phrases

(Repeat a different phrase for each of the 8 tapping points.)

(eyebrow) I choose to feel good about all that I have…

(side of eye) I love feeling safe with what I have earned…

(under eye) I love feeling free of the guilt…

(under nose) It's so nice to appreciate all that I have…

(chin) I'm happy I released the guilt…

(collarbone) I finally feel safe with what I have earned…

(under arm) I love feeling free of the guilt…

(head) I appreciate all that I have.

ISSUE: GUILT ABOUT WANTING MORE

Repeat the statement below out loud and measure *how true it feels* or how high your guilt is:

- *I feel guilty because I want more* _____ (0-10)

*(Repeat the following **setup statement** 3 times while tapping the **karate chop point**.)*

> *Even though **I feel guilty because I want more**...maybe I'm selfish...I deeply and completely accept myself anyway.*

ROUND #1: Negative Reminder Phrase

*(Repeat the following **reminder phrase** while tapping the sequence of 8 tapping points.)*

> *I feel guilty because I want more.*

Measure the guilt again on the 0-10 point **Intensity Scale**, and continue tapping until the feeling of guilt is significantly reduced. Then you may proceed to the positive phrases.

ROUND #2: Positive Phrases

(Repeat a different phrase for each of the 8 tapping points.)

(eyebrow) I appreciate all that I am...

(side of eye) I love knowing how generous I am...

(under eye) I can have desires and feel good about myself...

(under nose) I'm grateful for all my desires...

(chin) I am allowed to want...

(collarbone) I love knowing how generous I am...

(under arm) I can have desires and feel good about myself...

(head) I'm grateful for all my desires.

ISSUE: GUILT ABOUT ADVANTAGES

Many of my clients and people I've met in workshops feel guilty about having more advantages than others. Are you letting this guilt block you from attracting additional abundance?

- *I feel guilty because of the advantages I have* _____ (0-10)

*(Repeat the following **setup statement** 3 times while tapping the **karate chop point**.)*

---

*Even though **I feel guilty because of the advantages I have**, I choose to resolve this guilt now.*

ROUND #1: Negative Reminder Phrase

*(Repeat the following **reminder phrase** while tapping the sequence of 8 tapping points.)*

I feel guilty because of the advantages I have.

Measure the guilt again and notice how much it has decreased. If you are comfortable with where the **Intensity Scale** rating number is now, proceed to the positive phrase.

ROUND #2: Positive Phrases

(Repeat a different phrase for each of the 8 tapping points.)

(eyebrow) I accept all of me...

(side of eye) I love accepting who I am...

(under eye) I appreciate my entire life...

(under nose) I love feeling free of the conflict...

(chin) I accept that I have desires...

(collarbone) I love accepting who I am...

(under arm) I appreciate my entire life...

(head) I love feeling free of the conflict.

ISSUE: FEAR OF REJECTION

How high is your fear of being rejected? Say the following statement out loud and measure how fearful you are.

- ■ *I'm afraid they will reject me if I'm successful*
    _____ (0-10)

*(Repeat the following **setup statement** 3 times while tapping the **karate chop point**.)*

> *Even though **I'm afraid they will reject me if I become successful**, I completely love and accept who I am and how I feel.*

ROUND #1: Negative Reminder Phrase

*(Repeat the following **reminder phrase** while tapping the sequence of 8 tapping points.)*

> *I'm afraid they will reject me if I become successful.*

Where is your fear about being rejected on the 0-10 point scale now? Measure the level of fear by repeating the phrase out loud.

- ■ *I'm afraid they will reject me if I'm successful*
    _____ (0-10)

You may choose to either continue tapping for your fear, or proceed to the positive phrases below.

ROUND #2: Positive Phrases

(Repeat a different phrase for each of the 8 tapping points.)

(eyebrow) I choose to feel acceptable now...

(side of eye) I love accepting my success...

(under eye) I choose to release my need for their approval...

(under nose) I appreciate who I am...

(chin) I choose to feel acceptable inside myself...

(collarbone) I love accepting my success even if they don't...

(under arm) I choose to release my need for their approval...

(head) I appreciate how worthy I am.

ISSUE: REJECTING OTHERS

*(Repeat the following **setup statement** 3 times while tapping the **karate chop point**.)*

> *Even though **I'm afraid I might reject them if I get what I want**, I deeply and completely accept all of me.*

ROUND #1: Negative Reminder Phrase

*(Repeat the following **reminder phrase** while tapping the sequence of 8 tapping points.)*

> ***I'm afraid I might reject them if I get what I want.***

ROUND #2: Positive Phrases

(Repeat a different phrase for each of the 8 tapping points.)

(eyebrow) I love knowing I am enough as I am...

(side of eye) I love keeping the right friends...

(under eye) I love knowing I can trust myself...

(under nose) I appreciate how trustworthy I am...

(chin) I love knowing I can trust my friends...

(collarbone) I love keeping the right friends...

(under arm) I love trusting my instinct...

(head) I appreciate how trustworthy I am.

ISSUE: I'M AFRAID TO "ROCK THE BOAT"

Presumably, you want something now — better health, more money, a more suitable romantic partner — *because you think you'll feel better when the change occurs.*

If you do get the changes you are hoping for, how might your friends, family members and even colleagues change in reaction to you? What relationships could be threatened or thrown off balance? Are you afraid to *rock the boat*? Do you assume your newfound success will inevitably disturb the balance you are maintaining in one or more of your relationships?

Most people appreciate stability and enjoy being able to predict the behavior and reactions of others. Becoming enormously successful can change the balance of a friendship or family system and often feels threatening to one member of the relationship.

Ask yourself if it feels threatening to you that others may act and react differently if you become successful after years of experiencing struggle. This is different than the jealousy issue, and is simply about predictability and living with the known rather than the unknown.

Repeat the following statement out loud and measure your fear:

- *I'm afraid to rock the boat* _____ (0-10)

*(Repeat the following **setup statements** while tapping the **karate chop point**.)*

*Even though **I'm afraid to rock the boat and I'd rather everything stayed the same**, I deeply and profoundly love and accept myself anyway...Even **though I'm afraid they might react differently towards me if I change**, I accept who I am and how I feel...Even though **I'm convinced they'll react differently towards me if I change**, I deeply and completely accept myself anyway.*

ROUND #1: Negative Reminder Phrase

*(Repeat the following **reminder phrase** while tapping the sequence of 8 tapping points.)*

I'm afraid I'll rock the boat if I change...

Now repeat the phrase again and measure the intensity of your fear to see if it has been reduced.

- *I'm afraid I'll rock the boat if I change* _____ (0-10)

Has your fear decreased? You may continue tapping on this fear of rocking the boat, or proceed to the more positive solution-oriented statements.

ROUND #2: Positive Phrases

(Repeat a different phrase for each of the 8 tapping points.)

(eyebrow) I choose to accept them even if they react to me...

(side of eye) I can handle their reactions no matter what...

(under eye) I choose to accept my fears about this...

(under nose) I accept who I am and how I feel...

(chin) I choose to accept them even if they react to me...

(collarbone) I appreciate who I am and who they are...

(under arm) I choose to love and accept them even if they react...

(head) I feel confident and calm even though I'm changing.

ISSUE: I DON'T KNOW WHOM TO TRUST

It is quite common to fear being unable to trust the motives of others if your situation changes from one of poverty to one of great prosperity. A client of mine on the verge of becoming "famous" in certain circles said *"How will I know which friends to trust now? How will I be able to recognize those who like me for me rather than for my fame?"*

Could this fear be holding you back or causing you to sabotage your forward movement or momentum?

*(Repeat the following **setup statements** while tapping the **karate chop point**.)*

> *Even though **I don't know whom to trust now that I have attracted the abundance I have been wanting**, I deeply and completely love and accept all of me anyway...Even **though I don't know whom to trust now that I've changed so much**, I accept who I am and how I feel...Even **though I'm afraid to trust anyone now that I've changed**, I deeply and completely accept myself anyway.*

ROUND #1: Negative Reminder Phrase

*(Repeat the following **reminder phrase** while tapping the sequence of 8 tapping points.)*

I don't know whom to trust now that I'm so successful.

ROUND #2: Positive Phrases

(Repeat a different phrase for each of the 8 tapping points.)

(eyebrow) I choose to trust my gut instinct…

(side of eye) I accept that I will know who is trustworthy…

(under eye) I choose to accept myself even though I have fears…

(under nose) I deserve to trust others and be trusted…

(chin) I choose to recognize trustworthy friends…

(collarbone) I appreciate who I am and who they are…

(under arm) I will trust my inner wisdom…

(head) I choose to trust the right people.

Continue to use **EFT** on additional negative tapping sequences until the measurement of your emotional charge on the **Intensity Scale** has been reduced significantly on this issue.

ISSUE: FEAR OF ENVY

*(Repeat the following **setup statement** 3 times while tapping the **karate chop point**.)*

*Even though **I'm afraid they will envy me**, I choose to accept myself and mind my own business.*

ROUND #1: Negative Reminder Phrase

*(Repeat the following **reminder phrase** while tapping the sequence of 8 tapping points.)*

I'm afraid they will envy me.

ROUND #2: Positive Phrases

(Repeat a different phrase for each of the 8 tapping points.)

(eyebrow) I don't care if they are envious…

(side of eye) It's none of my business…

(under eye) I love feeling free…

(under nose) I accept my success now…

(chin) Their envy doesn't concern me…

(collarbone) It's none of my business…

(under arm) I love feeling free…

(head) I accept my success now.

ISSUE: STANDING OUT

It is likely that this phrase will trigger memories of a past event when you **DID** stand out, and didn't like the reaction from others.

Measure the emotional *charge* on this statement:

- *I'm afraid to stand out* _____ (0-10)

(Repeat the following setup statement 3 times while tapping the karate chop point.)

> Even though *I'm afraid to stand out*, I choose to accept myself and own my power now.

ROUND #1: Negative Reminder Phrase

(Repeat the following reminder phrase while tapping the sequence of 8 tapping points.)

> ### *I'm afraid to stand out.*

In other words, there may be good reasons you don't want to stand out! Measure the statement now, and notice what specific events surfaced *("the time I stood out and got in trouble...the time I stood out and they laughed at me...the time I stood out and I got criticized...")*

- ***I'm afraid to stand out*** _____ (0-10)

You may continue to tap on this fear of standing out, or switch the wording to target a specific event from your past. For instance, maybe you are remembering a time when you stood out and someone made fun of you. That would then become the target for your **EFT** tapping before advancing to tapping on the positive phrases.

ROUND #2: Positive Phrases

(Repeat a different phrase for each of the 8 tapping points.)

(eyebrow) I can stand out and feel safe…

(side of eye) I choose to feel safe even if I stand out…

(under eye) I love feeling safe with my success…

(under nose) I know it is right for me…

(chin) I can stand out and feel safe…

(collarbone) I choose to feel safe even if they don't like me…

(under arm) I love feeling safe with my success…

(head) I know it is right for me.

ISSUE: HUMILIATION

Since I have included the word "again" in my *Setup Statement* below, obviously I am assuming there was a past event that you will be tuning into that would make you feel reluctant to stand out.

Repeat this phrase out loud and measure the intensity on it.

- *I'm afraid they will humiliate me again* _____ (0-10)

*(Repeat the following **setup statement** 3 times while tapping the **karate chop point**.)*

> *Even though **I'm afraid they will humiliate me again** if I stand out, I deeply and completely love and accept myself anyway.*

ROUND #1: Negative Reminder Phrase

*(Repeat the following **reminder phrase** while tapping the sequence of 8 tapping points.)*

> *I'm afraid they will humiliate me again if I stand out.*

How true does this statement feel to you now that you have been tapping on it?

- *I'm afraid they will humiliate me again* _____ (0-10)

Now you have a choice. You could either continue tapping for the fear of their humiliating you again, or you could plug in the past event issue into your **Setup Statement**. For instance, your new **Setup Statement** might sound like this:

> *Even though **I remember how hurt I felt when they humiliated me last time**...I deeply and profoundly love and accept myself anyway.*

ROUND #2: Positive Phrases

(Repeat a different phrase for each of the 8 tapping points.)

(eyebrow) I've healed from that trauma...

(side of eye) I am safe now...

(under eye) I don't care what they think if I'm successful...

(under nose) It's safe to stand out...

(chin) I've healed from that trauma...

(collarbone) I am safe now inside myself...

(under arm) Their feelings are none of my business...

(head) It's safe to stand out in new ways.

ISSUE: FITTING IN

Repeat this statement out loud and measure *how true* it feels to you.

- *I'm afraid I won't fit in if I'm successful* _____ (0-10)

*(Repeat the following **setup statement** 3 times while tapping the **karate chop point**.)*

> *Even though **I'm afraid I won't fit in if I'm successful**, I accept who I am and how I feel.*

ROUND #1: Negative Reminder Phrase

*(Repeat the following **reminder phrase** while tapping the sequence of 8 tapping points.)*

> *I'm afraid I won't fit in if I'm successful.*

Repeat the phrase again and notice if the fear has been reduced.

- *I'm afraid I won't fit in if I'm successful* _____ (0-10)

You may either continue tapping on your fear until it is significantly reduced, or move on to the positive phrases.

ROUND #2: Positive Phrases

(Repeat a different phrase for each of the 8 tapping points.)

(eyebrow) I love knowing I fit in anyway...

(side of eye) I don't have to fit in with everyone...

(under eye) I choose to fit in now...

(under nose) I feel safe being different now...

(chin) I love knowing I fit in anyway...

(collarbone) I don't have to fit in with everyone...

(under arm) I choose to fit in now...

(head) I appreciate being different anyway.

ISSUE: WHAT IF THEY THINK I'M GREEDY?

*(Repeat the following **setup statement** 3 times while tapping the **karate chop point**.)*

> *Even though **I'm afraid they'll think I'm greedy if I am rich**, I deeply and completely accept myself and the abundance that's coming in.*

ROUND #1: Negative Reminder Phrase

*(Repeat the following **reminder phrase** while tapping the sequence of 8 tapping points.)*

> ***I'm afraid they'll think I'm greedy if I'm rich.***

ROUND #2: Positive Phrases

(Repeat a different phrase for each of the 8 tapping points.)

(eyebrow) I love feeling wealthy...

(side of eye) I love giving to others...

(under eye) I appreciate wealthy people...

(under nose) I look forward to giving back...

(chin) I love feeling wealthy...

(collarbone) I love giving to others...

(under arm) I appreciate wealthy people and their generosity...

(head) I can't wait to give back.

ISSUE: JEALOUSY

The only reason you wouldn't want others to be jealous of you when you are successful is because you have a past memory of someone acting out and being nasty as a result of feeling jealous! Repeat the phrase below out loud and measure the intensity or "truth" of it:

- *I'm afraid of their jealousy* _____ (0-10)

*(Repeat the following **setup statement** 3 times while tapping the **karate chop point**.)*

> *Even though **I'm afraid they will be jealous of me**, I choose to embrace the abundance in my life.*

ROUND #1: Negative Reminder Phrase

*(Repeat the following **reminder phrase** while tapping the sequence of 8 tapping points.)*

> *I'm afraid they will be jealous of me.*

Measure your fear of their jealousy again. Is it still high for you on the **Intensity Scale**?

- *I'm afraid they will be jealous of me* _____ (0-10)

If the fear has been reduced enough for you, you may choose a memory of a time when someone was jealous and nasty to you, and use the specifics of that story for a new **EFT** round. Otherwise, proceed to the positive phrases below.

ROUND #2: Positive Phrases

(Repeat a different phrase for each of the 8 tapping points.)

(eyebrow) They can be jealous and it's none of my business...

(side of eye) I choose to feel accepting of my feelings...

(under eye) I love feeling wealthy and enjoying it...

(under nose) I love the abundance in my life...

(chin) They can be jealous and it's none of my business...

(collarbone) I accept who I am...

(under arm) I love feeling wealthy and worthy...

(head) I love the abundance in my life.

ISSUE: INADEQUACY

Repeat the statement below out loud and measure *how true* it feels to you.

- *I feel "less than" and inadequate around wealthy people* _____ (0-10)

(Repeat the following setup statement 3 times while tapping the karate chop point.)

Even though I always feel "less than" and inadequate around wealthy people, I deeply and completely accept myself anyway.

ROUND #1: Negative Reminder Phrase

(Repeat the following reminder phrase while tapping the sequence of 8 tapping points.)

I feel "less than" around wealthy people.

Repeat the statement out loud again and measure *how true* it feels to you now:

- *I feel less than and inadequate around wealthy people* _____ (0-10)

Continue tapping while using the negative reminder phrase above until you feel confident that the rating of your emotional charge has dropped significantly on the 0-10 point **Intensity Scale**. Then proceed to the positive phrases below. If any specific events surface, use them as targets for additional rounds of **EFT**.

ROUND #2: Positive Phrases

(Repeat a different phrase for each of the 8 tapping points.)

(eyebrow) I am enough with the money I have...

(side of eye) They are enough...

(under eye) We all are enough...

(under nose) I am good enough as I am...

(chin) I am enough and I have plenty...

(collarbone) They are enough...

(under arm) We all are enough...

(head) I am good enough as I am.

COMFORT

ZONES

COMFORT ZONES

- **Are you stuck within a particular *comfort zone*?**

I didn't think I struggled with a **comfort zone** around my earning power until I added up my income two years running and found I had made nearly the ***exact*** same amount of money each year.

Given all the parameters and factors of managing a full-time private practice, this is almost impossible to accomplish. Clients took vacations, I took vacations, holidays fell on different days, new clients came in to my practice, old clients terminated, etc.

In other words, I was obviously struggling with a ***financial ceiling*** or **comfort zone** above which I was not willing to climb. Until, that is, I applied **EFT** to myself on my ***limiting beliefs***. I have roughly ***quadrupled my income*** in a few short years.

Try the following **EFT Setup Statements**. And remember:

- **All of the Setup Statements should be repeated 3 times while you *tap the karate chop point.***

- **The *highlighted phrases* should be repeated out loud while you tap the sequence of 8 points. Then tap the entire sequence of points again while repeating the positive phrases out loud.**

ISSUE: NEGATIVE BELIEFS

Repeat this statement out loud and measure *how true* it feels to you:

- *I'm convinced that I can't make more money*
  _____ (0-10)
    o Why not?
    o What's in your way?
    o Who's in your way?
    o Who taught you this?
    o Why do you believe this?

*(Repeat the following **setup statement** 3 times while tapping the **karate chop point**.)*

> Even though *I don't believe I can make more money*, I choose to release this block.

ROUND #1: Negative Reminder Phrase

*(Repeat the following **reminder phrase** while tapping the sequence of 8 tapping points.)*

> *I don't believe I can make more money.*

Does this still feel true to you? Has the charge been reduced on the "truth" of this? Continue tapping until it no longer feels true to you. Then proceed to the positive phrases.

ROUND #2: Positive Phrases

(Repeat a different phrase for each of the 8 tapping points.)

(eyebrow) My belief has changed…

(side of eye) Now I know I can make more money…

(under eye) I love feeling good earning a higher salary…

(under nose) I love knowing I resolved this conflict…

(chin) My belief has changed…

(collarbone) I'm already making more money…

(under arm) I love feeling good earning a higher salary…

(head) I feel so secure knowing I resolved this conflict.

ISSUE: FEAR OF EARNING MORE

Why would you be afraid of earning more money? What supports this fear for you? Say the statement below out loud and measure how high your fear is.

- *I'm afraid to make more money* _____ (0-10)

*(Repeat the following **setup statement** 3 times while tapping the **karate chop point**.)*

> *Even though **I'm afraid to make more money**, I deeply and completely accept myself.*

ROUND #1: Negative Reminder Phrase

*(Repeat the following **reminder phrase** while tapping the sequence of 8 tapping points.)*

> *I'm afraid to make more money.*

Are you still as afraid to make more money? Did memories surface that would support this fear? Continue tapping on the *"fear of making more money"* until it no longer bothers you. This will change your **vibration** about money and I expect that you will see a difference in your annual earnings.

98

ROUND #2: Positive Phrases

(Repeat a different phrase for each of the 8 tapping points.)

(eyebrow) I feel safe making more money...

(side of eye) I know it is right for me...

(under eye) I choose to trust myself...

(under nose) I choose to feel good about my salary...

(chin) I allow myself to feel safe making more money...

(collarbone) I know it is right for me to earn more...

(under arm) I choose to trust myself...

(head) I choose to feel good about increasing my salary.

ISSUE: COMFORT ZONE AROUND SALARY

*(Repeat the following **setup statement** 3 times while tapping the **karate chop point**.)*

*Even though **I'm limited by a comfort zone around my current salary**, I deeply and completely accept myself anyway.*

ROUND #1: Negative Reminder Phrase

*(Repeat the following **reminder phrase** while tapping the sequence of 8 tapping points.)*

I'm limited by a comfort zone around my current salary.

ROUND #2: Positive Phrases

(Repeat a different phrase for each of the 8 tapping points.)

(eyebrow) I'm so happy I expanded my comfort zone...

(side of eye) I love knowing I am in control...

(under eye) I appreciate all of my power...

(under nose) I love knowing I expanded my comfort zone...

(chin) I'm grateful I expanded my comfort zone...

(collarbone) I am increasing my salary already...

(under arm) I appreciate and understand my power...

(head) I love knowing my comfort zone has expanded.

ABUNDANCE GAMES

THE GUESS WHAT LETTER

The **GUESS WHAT LETTER** is a really fun game that combines *visualization* with *intense emotion* to help you *vibrate* in a joyful place that will help you *attract easily* what you have been asking for into your life.

Write a letter to a team of supporters, a friend, a mentor, or someone very important in your life who would be *extremely* excited about your success.

Dear Lisa,

Guess what? You won't believe it. I was asked by a huge multi-national company to conduct their in-house coaching with EFT for stress management! They are willing to pay me more money a week than I usually make in a month! I am so excited it's hard to sleep at night. They want me to start immediately and are flying me first class to their headquarters for an introductory meeting with their staff.

> *I just wanted you to be the first to know. Thanks for all your support this year. It has meant the world to me.*
>
> *Love, Carol*

Write a different letter every day, playing with the outcome and shaping the details of what you *intend* to *attract* into your life. I used the *TELEPHONE TECHNIQUE*, a version of the letter, when I wanted to increase my business enough to have a waiting list. Out loud, I pretended I was leaving a message on a friend's machine:

> *"Hi, it's Carol. I just wanted to let you know I am overwhelmed with business and now have a waiting list a mile long! No more wondering if clients are going to show up or not. Call me soon. I need to refer you lots of clients."*

DAILY GRATITUDE JOURNAL

I recommend that you keep a **DAILY GRATITUDE JOURNAL**. I make time every day to write for about ten minutes in this journal. I write a list of everything I feel *grateful* for, everything I enjoy in my life, and every friend, loved one and pet that I appreciate. Keeping a journal doesn't take much time, and in my personal experience, yields amazingly fast results. In fact, sometimes I feel spooked by just how quickly something wonderful comes into my life when I am focusing on the *joyful feelings of gratitude* and *appreciation*.

Try it, I guarantee you will have exciting results!

One of the first times I took this exercise seriously, I sat down at the table and started writing a list of everything I felt grateful for in my life, no matter how small or large. In essence, I was *counting my blessings*. If I thought of something that I felt I *should* be grateful for, but honestly wasn't, I left it off my list.

I had turned down the volume on my answering machine during this exercise. When I had finished with my list, I saw that my machine was blinking and I listened to the message that came through when I had been absorbed in my journal. The message was from a former client, calling from California, saying she had finally gotten it together enough to send me the $1,500 that she had owed me (from bouncing several checks and replacing them with more bounced checks) *and that I could expect to receive it any day*. That's how fast it worked for me…you can call it a *coincidence* if you like, I don't care. I hope to have many more coincidences like that!

Make the *choice* to put aside ten minutes a day for yourself. You're worth it.

Let's continue releasing the blocks on your path to *attracting* what you want in your life.

STEP #2

INCREASE

YOUR

PROSPERITY

CONSCIOUSNESS

STEP #2
INCREASE YOUR
PROSPERITY CONSCIOUSNESS

Our *consciousness* is reflected in our outside world of financial success, material comforts, bodily health and relationships. If your consciousness is one of *SCARCITY*, you will find that finances (or good relationships) are lacking in your life. If you answer *YES* to any of the questions in this section, it is likely that you need to work on building your *Prosperity Consciousness* so that you can allow more *abundance* into your life. With **EFT**, you can work on this daily.

- **Do you feel afraid that if you have *more money*, you will be taking away from others?**

Many people think there is a finite amount of money in the world, and that if they increase their annual salary, they are actually *taking money away* from someone else. Since they were taught not to be selfish, they resist (unconsciously) earning more money.

- **Do you feel afraid that your *supply* (of money, food, resources) will run out?**

"Janet" truly believed there would always be shortages of some kind. She had grown up with fearful parents, even though there was always enough food and enough resources so she and her siblings didn't feel lack. What she absorbed was her parents' anxiety around money. Janet's mother continues to use the teabag twice...just in case there won't be enough later.

- **Do you find yourself hoarding money in case of an emergency?**

Too many people hoard their money for a future rainy day. But believe me, hoarders don't use their money on a rainy day either. Instead, they stay inside and count their cash! When you are afraid that your supply will run out, you are actually *emitting a powerful signal* of fear that *repels abundance*. Remember, whatever *signal you are emitting* will *magnetize* back to you the same energy, in this case, fear and lack of resources.

- **Do your thoughts of lack or scarcity block your receiving?**

Many people have difficulty *receiving*, partly because they are convinced there isn't enough, and partly because they were taught it is more generous to give. Consider

"Melanie" who rejected gifts, compliments and money from anyone who tried to give to her. In fact it was very selfish of her *NOT* to receive, and rather self-centered. Many people told her they were hurt by her inability to accept what they offered her.

If you want to increase your *Prosperity Consciousness*, and therefore draw more *prosperity* into your life, continue with the **EFT** tapping exercises below.

I believe in being generous according to your ability. Unless you are destitute, I recommend you choose meaningful charities and give them annual gifts. The *energy of giving and receiving* needs to remain smooth and balanced.

In this section, I provide **3** *Setup Statements* for you to say out loud while you are tapping the **karate chop point**. Choose whichever *highlighted phrase* most fits your feeling, (or repeat the phrase I have placed in the box) during your first round of **EFT**.

ISSUE: I'M CONVINCED MONEY/WEALTH IS "BAD"

Are you? Who taught you that money is bad or evil? What was the proof or evidence they gave you? Does it sound reasonable right now when you state this out loud? How true does it feel when you repeat the following statements?

- *Money is evil* _____ (0-10)
- *Being wealthy is bad* _____ (0-10)
- *I shouldn't want more of it* _____ (0-10)

Of course the most often misquoted biblical expression is *"the love of money is the root of all evil"* and we have ended up interpreting this to mean *"money is the root of all evil."* Money, simply an energy of exchange, isn't bad by itself...but chasing money, following financial pursuits for the wrong reasons, valuing money above love, friendship or integrity is not a way I choose to live my life and I would never recommend anyone I know do it either.

One of my clients said his parents had contempt for their rich cousins, and often said *"at least we're the happy ones."* So he interpreted the prospect of becoming wealthy as a threat to losing his peace of mind and happiness. Money can never be equated with happiness.

Say the following statement out loud and measure how true it feels to you on the 0-10 point **Intensity Scale**:

- *I'm convinced money is bad* _____ (0-10)

*(Repeat the following **setup statements** while tapping the **karate chop point**.)*

> *Even though **I'm convinced money is bad**, I accept who I am and what I was taught...Even though **they taught me that money is evil**, I choose to accept who I am and how I feel...Even though **my parents thought money was bad**, I choose to accept who I am and how I feel.*

ROUND #1: Negative Reminder Phrase

*(Repeat the following **reminder phrase** while tapping the sequence of 8 tapping points.)*

> *I'm convinced (having) money is bad.*

Measure the statement again and notice whether your inherited conviction about money has loosened up a bit.

- *I'm convinced money is bad* _____ (0-10)

You may continue tapping on this conviction until the "truth" of it has been reduced significantly, or continue with the positive phrases below.

ROUND #2: Positive Phrases

(Repeat a different phrase for each of the 8 tapping points.)

(eyebrow) I accept that money is only energy…

(side of eye) I choose to have my own beliefs…

(under eye) I choose a new belief about money…

(under nose) I deserve to believe that money is only energy…

(chin) I accept all of me and choose a new belief…

(collarbone) Money is neutral and I accept it…

(under arm) I choose to feel peaceful about money…

(head) I feel calm and peaceful about having money.

Continue with subsequent tapping rounds until the "truth" of the statement – *"I believe money is bad/evil"* drops down to a 1 or 0.

ISSUE: IT'S NOT SAFE TO RELAX ABOUT MONEY

My client "John" was wealthy by most standards. He had a solid savings amount in his bank account, plenty of investments, and a good position at work that was practically guaranteed for the next several years. However, his parents, who had experienced several decades of lean years, taught him to never relax about money, constantly reminding him that something catastrophic could happen if he relaxed his watchful eye on his investments. They actually encouraged him to worry relentlessly, regardless of the amount he had saved or the income stream he was earning. His father, speaking from his own experience, often warned him, *"It could disappear instantly if you're not watching carefully."*

Rate the "truth" of the following statements:

- ***It's not safe to relax about money*_____ (0-10)**
- ***Money can disappear at any moment*_____ (0-10)**
- ***I can't let down my guard about money*_____ (0-10)**

After getting your 0-10 point measurement on these above statements, use these words in the negative tapping round.

*(Repeat the following **setup statements** while tapping the **karate chop point**.)*

---

*Even though **I have to be vigilant about my money**, I deeply and profoundly love and accept myself anyway...Even though **I can never relax about money**, I deeply and completely love and accept my feelings...Even though **I must stay alert at all times about my finances**, I accept who I am and how I feel.*

ROUND #1: Negative Reminder Phrase

*(Repeat the following **reminder phrase** while tapping the sequence of 8 tapping points.)*

It's not safe to relax about money.

ROUND #2: Positive Phrases

(Repeat a different phrase for each of the 8 tapping points.)

(eyebrow) I choose to start relaxing about money matters…

(side of eye) I love feeling more relaxed about my money…

(under eye) I choose to relax and still make smart decisions...

(under nose) I want to relax about money…

(chin) I choose to relax and still make the right decisions...

(collarbone) I appreciate my finances now…

(under arm) I love knowing I can relax now…

(head) I feel relaxed and confident about money.

ISSUE: DESERVING ABUNDANCE

Say the following statement out loud and measure *how true* it feels to you.

- *I don't deserve more than they have* _____ (0-10)

*(Repeat the following **setup statements** while tapping the **karate chop point**.)*

> *Even though **I don't deserve more than they have**, I deeply and completely accept who I am...Even though **I don't want to take it away from others**, I choose to accept myself anyway...Even though **I feel selfish having these desires**, I am enough now.*

ROUND #1: Negative Reminder Phrase

*(Repeat the following **reminder phrase** while tapping the sequence of 8 tapping points.)*

> ***I feel selfish taking away from others and I don't deserve it.***

ROUND #2: Positive Phrases

(Repeat a different phrase for each of the 8 tapping points.)

(eyebrow) I deserve more than enough…

(side of eye) So do they…

(under eye) There is enough for everyone…

(under nose) I am entitled to plenty and so are they…

(chin) We all deserve more than enough…

(collarbone) And there is enough for all of us…

(under arm) There is enough for everyone…

(head) I am entitled to plenty.

ISSUE: NOT ENOUGH/ SHORTAGES

*(Repeat the following **setup statements** while tapping the **karate chop point**.)*

*Even though **there's not enough for everyone**, I choose to believe in plenty...Even though **there has never been enough in my family**, I choose to change this belief...Even though **I'm afraid there will always be shortages**, I completely accept myself anyway.*

ROUND #1: Negative Reminder Phrase

*(Repeat the following **reminder phrase** while tapping the sequence of 8 tapping points.)*

I'm afraid there will always be shortages.

ROUND #2: Positive Phrases

(Repeat a different phrase for each of the 8 tapping points.)

(eyebrow) There is enough...

(side of eye) We can all have enough...

(under eye) There is more than enough...

(under nose) I accept my desires...

(chin) There is enough for everyone...

(collarbone) There is plenty for all of us...

(under arm) There is more than enough...

(head) I accept my healthy desires for more.

ISSUE: MONEY WORRIES

Measure how true these statements are for you:

- ■ *I should worry about money all the time* _____ (0-10)
- ■ *It would be irresponsible not to worry* _____ (0-10)

*(Repeat the following **setup statements** while tapping the **karate chop point**.)*

---

*Even though **I believe I should worry about money**, I deeply and completely accept my feelings anyway...Even though **I'd be irresponsible if I didn't worry about money**, I choose to feel more relaxed about it now...Even though **I'm afraid to let down my guard**, I accept all of me anyway.*

ROUND #1: Negative Reminder Phrase

*(Repeat the following **reminder phrase** while tapping the sequence of 8 tapping points.)*

I'd be irresponsible if I didn't worry about money.

Repeat the following statement again and measure how true it feels to you now:

- *It's irresponsible not to worry about money*
  _____ (0-10)

Continue tapping on this issue or the other fears you have about letting down your guard. Then proceed to the positive phrases below.

ROUND #2: Positive Phrases

(Repeat a different phrase for each of the 8 tapping points.)

(eyebrow) I intend to relax about money...

(side of eye) I love feeling easy about money...

(under eye) There will be enough...

(under nose) There is enough already...

(chin) I intend to feel more relaxed about money...

(collarbone) I love feeling easy about money...

(under arm) There is already enough...

(head) There is enough now.

ISSUE: SUPPLY/ RUNNING OUT

This feeling of urgency about a particular supply running out is common for people struggling with abundance issues in their lives. I recommend testing the "truth" of this statement or the amount of fear present, and then searching for specific events that may support this fear:

- ***I'm afraid I'll run out...there isn't enough*** _____ (0-10)
    - o Where did you get this idea that there wasn't enough?
    - o How did you learn this?
    - o What did your family say that taught you this fear?
    - o When have you experienced it in the past?

The answers to these questions could be formulated into new ***Setup Statements*** for **EFT**.

*(Repeat the following **setup statements** while tapping the **karate chop point**.)*

---

*Even though **I'm afraid I'll run out**, I choose to feel relaxed now...Even though **I might run out of what I need**, I accept how I feel...Even though **there isn't enough sometimes**, I choose to believe in prosperity.*

ROUND #1: Negative Reminder Phrase

*(Repeat the following **reminder phrase** while tapping the sequence of 8 tapping points.)*

> ### *I'm afraid I'll run out because there isn't enough.*

Do you still feel afraid that you will run out? Does it still feel true that there will never be enough?

- ### *I'm afraid I'll run out... there isn't enough* _____ (0-10)

Continue tapping on this fear and belief until it feels right for you to move on to the positive statements below.

ROUND #2: Positive Phrases

(Repeat a different phrase for each of the 8 tapping points.)

> *(eyebrow) I have enough now...*
>
> *(side of eye) There will always be more...*
>
> *(under eye) I love knowing I am safe...*
>
> *(under nose) I love knowing there is enough...*
>
> *(chin) I don't need to run out...*
>
> *(collarbone) There will always be more...*
>
> *(under arm) I love knowing I am being taken care of...*
>
> *(head) I love knowing there is enough.*

ISSUE: THERE WILL NEVER BE ENOUGH

This next statement is much stronger than the previous one, and is categorized as a true "conviction." Repeat the phrase out loud and measure *how true* it feels to you now:

- ■ *I'm convinced there will NEVER be enough* _____ (0-10)

*(Repeat the following **setup statements** while tapping the **karate chop point.**)*

> *Even though **I'm convinced there will never be enough**, I deeply and completely accept that there is plenty...Even though **there's never enough for me**, I choose to relax about this subject...Even though **my belief in scarcity is very, very strong**, I intend to release it now.*

ROUND #1: Negative Reminder Phrase

*(Repeat the following **reminder phrase** while tapping the sequence of 8 tapping points.)*

> *I'm convinced there will never be enough.*

Does this still feel as true as when you measured it before the tapping? Say the statement out loud again to measure the "truth" of it. Continue tapping until it doesn't feel as true, or until you discover the underlying specific events or incidents you heard or witnessed that made you believe this.

ROUND #2: Positive Phrases

(Repeat a different phrase for each of the 8 tapping points.)

(eyebrow) There is enough already...

(side of eye) There will be enough...

(under eye) Those lean times are over...

(under nose) I believe in prosperity now...

(chin) There is enough already...

(collarbone) There will be enough...

(under arm) I feel abundance everywhere...

(head) I believe in prosperity now.

ISSUE: I DON'T BELIEVE IN PROSPERITY

What do you mean *"I don't believe in prosperity"*? Why not? Who taught you that **prosperity** is a concept that isn't worth believing?

State the phrase below out loud and measure *how true* it feels to you on the 0-10 point **Intensity Scale**.

- *I don't believe in prosperity* _____ (0-10)

*(Repeat the following **setup statements** while tapping the **karate chop point**.)*

Even though *I don't believe in prosperity*, I choose to believe in abundance today...Even though *I don't feel safe believing there is enough*, I accept how I am feeling...Even though *it feels foolish to believe in prosperity*, I choose to believe in it now.

ROUND #1: Negative Reminder Phrase

*(Repeat the following **reminder phrase** while tapping the sequence of 8 tapping points.)*

I don't believe in prosperity.

Say the phrase again out loud and measure the "truth" of it to see if the rating on the 0-10 point **Intensity Scale** has been reduced.

- ***I don't believe in prosperity*** _____ (0-10)

Continue tapping on the above phrase or move on to the more positive, solution-oriented phrases provided below.

ROUND #2: Positive Phrases

(Repeat a different phrase for each of the 8 tapping points.)

(eyebrow) There is enough now...

(side of eye) There is plenty for all of us...

(under eye) I appreciate the feeling of abundance...

(under nose) I choose success now...

(chin) There is enough now...

(collarbone) There is plenty for all of us...

(under arm) I appreciate the feeling of abundance...

(head) I choose success now.

ISSUE: BELIEF IN SCARCITY

*(Repeat the following **setup statements** while tapping the **karate chop point**.)*

*Even though **I believe in scarcity**, I completely accept my thoughts and feelings… Even though **I inherited this fear from my family**, I choose to release it now…Even though **I'm not willing to release the fear**, I choose to accept who I am.*

ROUND #1: Negative Reminder Phrase

*(Repeat the following **reminder phrase** while tapping the sequence of 8 tapping points.)*

I believe in scarcity and I'm not willing to release this fear.

ROUND #2: Positive Phrases

(Repeat a different phrase for each of the 8 tapping points.)

(eyebrow) I choose to release the fear...

(side of eye) The fear isn't mine...

(under eye) I love feeling free of the fear...

(under nose) I choose to believe in prosperity...

(chin) I choose to release the fear...

(collarbone) The fear isn't mine...

(under arm) I love feeling free of the fear...

(head) I choose to believe in prosperity already.

ISSUE: BLOCKS TO RECEIVING

Being able to receive is an enormous and integral part of the abundance picture. Why don't you think it's good to receive? Who taught you this? Is it only good to give?

- ***I don't think it's good to receive*** _____ (0-10)

*(Repeat the following **setup statements** while tapping the **karate chop point**.)*

---

*Even though **I have trouble receiving**, I choose to open up now...Even though **I don't think it's good to receive**, I have decided to receive with open arms...Even though **I'm afraid to receive**, I choose to feel relaxed and calm about money.*

ROUND #1: Negative Reminder Phrase

*(Repeat the following **reminder phrase** while tapping the sequence of 8 tapping points.)*

I don't think it's good to receive.

Did this belief loosen up after tapping? Repeat the statement out loud again and measure the "truth" of it. Continue tapping to reduce it more, or proceed to the positive phrases below.

ROUND #2: Positive Phrases:

(Repeat a different phrase for each of the 8 tapping points.)

(eyebrow) I choose to receive easily...

(side of eye) I am allowed to receive as you are...

(under eye) I love receiving and giving...

(under nose) Receiving is good for all of us...

(chin) I choose to receive with grace...

(collarbone) I am allowed to receive and so are you...

(under arm) I love receiving and giving...

(head) Receiving is good for all of us.

ISSUE: CONFLICT ABOUT RECEIVING

When we have a *conflict* about receiving, it is different than a straightforward block. A conflict implies you have a part of you that wants to receive and another part that thinks it is wrong.

*(Repeat the following **setup statements** while tapping the **karate chop point**.)*

> *Even though **they taught me to give instead of receive**, I choose to believe there is prosperity all around me...Even though **I haven't been able to receive in the past**, I choose to receive graciously now...Even though **I'm afraid they'll think I'm selfish**, I choose to know when it's right to receive.*

ROUND #1: Negative Reminder Phrase

*(Repeat the following **reminder phrase** while tapping the sequence of 8 tapping points.)*

> *I'm afraid they'll think I'm selfish if I receive.*

ROUND #2: Positive Phrases

(Repeat a different phrase for each of the 8 tapping points.)

(eyebrow) The past is over now...

(side of eye) I love receiving graciously...

(under eye) I choose to receive when I am offered love...

(under nose) I love receiving and giving...

(chin) The conflict is in my past...

(collarbone) I receive graciously...

(under arm) I choose to receive when I am offered love...

(head) I love receiving and giving.

ISSUE: WHO WILL I BE
IF I GET WHAT I WANT?

Identity issues usually surface when we try to change something about ourselves, even something we strongly desire. The familiar "old" self feels threatened by the unfamiliar "new" self even though it's who we say we want to become.

- Who will you be if you attract all the abundance you've been wanting?
- Does the change feel threatening to you inside?
- How will your personality change?
- Will you act differently towards others?
- Will they act differently towards you?
- What expectations are you afraid of from yourself? From others?

On the 0-10 point **Intensity Scale**, rate the "truth" of this statement when you say it out loud:

- *I won't know who I will be if I get what I want*
  _____ (0-10)

*(Repeat the following **setup statements** while tapping the **karate chop point**.)*

*Even though **I'm afraid I'll change too much if I get what I want**, I deeply and completely love and accept myself anyway...Even **though I won't recognize myself if I become wealthy after all these years of scarcity**, I choose to accept and appreciate that I have changed...Even though **I won't know who I am if I change and finally get what I want**, I accept who I am and these fears that I have.*

ROUND #1: Negative Reminder Phrase

*(Repeat the following **reminder phrase** while tapping the sequence of 8 tapping points.)*

I'm afraid I won't know who I will be if I get what I want...

ROUND #2: Positive Phrases

(Repeat a different phrase for each of the 8 tapping points.)

(eyebrow) I won't know who I am anymore...

(side of eye) Who will I be if I change?

(under eye) Who will I be if I get what I want?

(under nose) I won't know who I really am...

(chin) Changing scares me even though I want it...

(collarbone) I'm afraid to change...

(under arm) I won't recognize myself...

(head) What if they change too?

Measure the "truth" of the statement again, and proceed with additional tapping rounds as necessary.

ABUNDANCE GAMES

CASH COMFORT

Take a very crisp $50 or $100 bill and hold it in your hand. Turn it over, feel it, really sense the value of it. Notice the feelings that are coming up. Do you feel nervous? Strange? Unworthy? *Tap the sequence of points while you are staring at the bill and holding it.* Notice the anxiety disappearing, and keep track of other emotions that surface. Keep tapping until holding this amount of money in your hand feels *normal*.

Then try this exercise with a check made payable to yourself in the amount of $25,000. Write it out from your regular checking account. Look at it, note the feelings that surface, and *keep tapping until it is very believable that you deserve to have this amount.* Proceed to larger amounts such as $100,000, $500,000 and $1,000,000 until you know this is not only *possible*, but *probable* that these amounts will flow easily into your life.

GRATITUDE WALK

As you walk to work, walk the dog, do your daily errands and chores, or take a nature walk, notice what you like about your environment and announce it out loud. Then *count your blessings out loud*. Tell the universe what you love about your life. This habit will keep you at a higher *vibration of gratitude* and will release the resistance you have on an energetic level.

On one of my gratitude walks several summers ago, I became very enthusiastic about *raising my vibration*, and for 30 minutes I declared out loud with passion all that I was *grateful* for over and over again. Of course the list grew as I walked and pumped my arms. Three days later **EFT** founder Gary Craig called me and asked me if I wanted to teach a class with him in Connecticut. *Another coincidence, you say?* I wouldn't mind more of these fabulous coincidences in my life.

STEP #3

ACTIVATE

THE

LAW OF

ATTRACTION

STEP #3
ACTIVATE THE
LAW OF ATTRACTION

Actually, the *LAW of ATTRACTION* is always activated in your life. This law refers to an *energetic formula*: whatever you focus on, you will *attract* into your life. So if you are worried about all your bills, or aches and pains, or how people don't like you, you will be *attracting* more of those limitations into your daily life.

Chances are, if you answer *YES* to any of the questions in this section, you are frustrated with problems that continue to show up in your life, in spite of your *strong desire* to be successful. Fortunately, with **EFT** you can help yourself turn your focus around so you *activate the positive* and *attract an abundance of resources* rather than more of your worries.

Remember: we are *energetic* beings—just like little magnets—*attracting* anything we focus on into our lives. If you are *vibrating* about worry, you will attract more worrisome issues. If you feel abundant, you will attract more *abundance* and ease into your life on any subject.

- **Do you find yourself worrying all the time about how many expenses you have?**

"Karen" obsessed all day long about wanting more money. Her focus was not, however, on money, it was on the *lack* of money in her life. She thought about her pile of bills and worried about how she would pay them by juggling her paychecks, and unwittingly attracted more *lack* into her life in this way.

ISSUE: MONEY ANXIETY

If I can help you reduce the anxiety you have about the topic of money, you will be able to think clearly and make better financial decisions. If you can clear up your "energy" around the subject of money, more ideas and opportunities will tend to present themselves to you.

Repeat the phrase below out loud and measure how high your anxiety is about money:

- *I feel anxious when I think about money* _____ (0-10)

*(Repeat the following **setup statements** while tapping the **karate chop point**.)*

---

*Even though **I feel so anxious when I think of money**, I choose to feel more relaxed about it now...Even though **I'm afraid to open my bills**, I choose to believe in my ability to pay them...Even though **money concerns haunt me**, I choose to release my fears.*

ROUND #1: Negative Reminder Phrase

*(Repeat the following **reminder phrase** while tapping the sequence of 8 tapping points.)*

I feel so anxious when I think of money.

Repeat the phrase and test where your anxiety level is now. Continue tapping until the anxiety is reduced significantly, or proceed to the positive phrases below.

- *I feel anxious when I think about money* _____ (0-10)

ROUND #2: Positive Phrases

(Repeat a different phrase for each of the 8 tapping points.)

(eyebrow) I feel relaxed about money...

(side of eye) I feel free when I think of paying my bills...

(under eye) I am grateful for all the money in my life...

(under nose) I feel wealthy already...

(chin) I feel relaxed about money...

(collarbone) I feel free to pay my bills...

(under arm) I am grateful for all the money in my life...

(head) I feel wealthy now.

ISSUE: SCARCITY OF MONEY

Repeat these phrases and measure *how true* they feel on the 0-10 point **Intensity Scale**:

- *I don't have enough* _____ (0-10)

- *There will never be enough* _____ (0-10)

- *I worry about how little I have* _____ (0-10)

*(Repeat the following **setup statements** while tapping the **karate chop point**.)*

> Even though **I'm convinced I don't have what I need**, I choose to feel safe now anyway...Even though **I'm always worrying about how little money I have**, I choose to feel calm and relaxed...Even **though I don't know if I will be able to make ends meet**, I choose to feel relaxed and trust my ability to attract abundance.

ROUND #1: Negative Reminder Phrase

*(Repeat the following **reminder phrase** while tapping the sequence of 8 tapping points.)*

> **I'm always worrying about how little money I have.**

ROUND #2: Positive Phrases

(Repeat a different phrase for each of the 8 tapping points.)

(eyebrow) I do have what I need already...

(side of eye) I love feeling satisfied...

(under eye) I have a lot of money...

(under nose) I have always made ends meet...

(chin) I do have what I need now...

(collarbone) I am satisfied now...

(under arm) I have plenty in my life...

(head) I love feeling abundant.

ISSUE: MONEY DOESN'T COME EASILY

This statement may honestly reflect your past experience, but it doesn't have to predict the future. If you can change your energy around this belief, you can change your external circumstances. Remember *beliefs precede manifestations* when we use the *Law of Attraction*.

*(Repeat the following **setup statements** while tapping the **karate chop point**.)*

---

*Even though **money has never come easily to me, and probably never will**, I choose to feel relaxed now…Even though **I don't expect myself to pay my bills**, I know that my situation is changing now…Even **though money has never come easily to me**, I have decided to change this pattern.*

ROUND #1: Negative Reminder Phrase

*(Repeat the following **reminder phrase** while tapping the sequence of 8 tapping points.)*

Money has never come easily to me.

ROUND #2: Positive Phrases

(Repeat a different phrase for each of the 8 tapping points.)

(eyebrow) Money is coming easily to me now...

(side of eye) I am increasing my prosperity consciousness...

(under eye) I am so happy that I attract money easily now...

(under nose) Thank you Spirit for opening these channels...

(chin) Money is coming easily to me now...

(collarbone) I love my new prosperity consciousness...

(under arm) I am so happy that I attract money so easily...

(head) Thank you Spirit for opening so many channels.

- **Do you feel certain your life will be much better when you earn more money?**

- **Are you convinced you can't be happy *until the bills are paid*, or until you have more money?**

If you are having trouble being happy in your day to day life *because of not having enough money*, you will be forever waiting for financial abundance. This is the *NOT UNTIL* illness.

Your assignment is to find ways to enjoy today, even if you are poor (or single or sick or unhappy). Finding reasons to feel better and thoughts that make you feel happier will bring the money, the success, good health, or whatever you are looking for, into your life faster.

Remember, we will ***attract back to us*** a match for the ***signal*** we are ***putting out*** to the universe. There are no exceptions to this ***Law of Attraction***. So even if it is an economic fact that you are poor, you must find a way to ***feel rich*** about something else in your life in order to raise your ***vibration*** and increase the positive manifestations in your life.

Many people resist this idea of focusing on a ***positive vibration***. They feel compelled to focus on how to make more money, what to do differently, and how to improve their advertising strategies. This is a trap and does not yield the results that improving your ***energetic vibration*** does.

If you would like to save time, and *attract* what you want faster, *change your energy* instead of your marketing plan.

Try the following **EFT Exercises**…

ISSUE: CAN'T BE HAPPY UNTIL...

Do you really believe this? Are you unhappy now because you don't have enough money? What could you focus on now that would make you happy?

Repeat this belief out loud and measure *how true* it feels to you on the 0-10 point **Intensity Scale**:

- *I can't be happy until I am wealthy* _____ (0-10)

(Repeat the following setup statement 3 times while tapping the karate chop point.)

Even though I don't believe I can be happy until I am wealthy, I choose to find things to be happy about now.

ROUND #1: Negative Reminder Phrase

(Repeat the following reminder phrase while tapping the sequence of 8 tapping points.)

I don't believe I can be happy until I am wealthy.

How does this statement feel to you now? Just as true? Hopefully it has loosened its grip on you as a result of the tapping. You may continue tapping on the negative feelings about this issue or proceed to the positive tapping round below.

ROUND #2: Positive Phrases

(Repeat a different phrase for each of the 8 tapping points.)

(eyebrow) I love being happy no matter how wealthy I am...

(side of eye) I appreciate all that I have in my life...

(under eye) I am happy now...

(under nose) I love expecting abundance in my life...

(chin) I love being happy now...

(collarbone) I appreciate all that I have in my life...

(under arm) I am happy now...

(head) I expect abundance in my life.

ISSUE: CAN'T FEEL GOOD UNTIL...

Again, this is one of those "slippery slopes" of fears and convictions. It's not true that you can't feel good until you're relaxed about money, but it may be true that you have chosen this focus. Say the statement below out loud and honestly measure *how true* it feels to you:

- *I can't feel good until I relax about money*
  _____ (0-10)

*(Repeat the following **setup statement** 3 times while tapping the **karate chop point**.)*

> Even though *I can't feel good until I relax about money*, *I choose to feel relaxed and hopeful anyway...*

ROUND #1: Negative Reminder Phrase

*(Repeat the following **reminder phrase** while tapping the sequence of 8 tapping points.)*

> *I can't feel good until I relax about money.*

Does this statement still feel *as true* as it did before you started tapping? Tap another round until it decreases even more, or continue with the positive phrases below.

ROUND #2: Positive Phrases

(Repeat a different phrase for each of the 8 tapping points.)

(eyebrow) I am relaxed about money…

(side of eye) I finally understand it's easy to earn money…

(under eye) I appreciate knowing there will be enough…

(under nose) I intend to feel relaxed about money…

(chin) I feel taken care of…

(collarbone) I finally understand making money is easy…

(under arm) I appreciate knowing there is enough already…

(head) I intend to feel relaxed about money.

ISSUE: CAN'T BE HAPPY IF I'M POOR

This is actually up to you...I know there are issues we could all focus on that make us unhappy when we don't have what we want. In addition, there are topics we can focus on that make us feel happy, regardless of our financial circumstances.

- ***I can't be poor and happy*** _____ (0-10)

*(Repeat the following **setup statement** 3 times while tapping the **karate chop point**.)*

> *Even though **I can't be poor and happy**, I deeply and completely accept who I am now.*

ROUND #1: Negative Reminder Phrase

*(Repeat the following **reminder phrase** while tapping the sequence of 8 tapping points.)*

> ***I can't be poor and happy.***

ROUND #2: Positive Phrases

(Repeat a different phrase for each of the 8 tapping points.)

(eyebrow) I am happy now anyway…

(side of eye) I love feeling good…

(under eye) I am wealthy in spirit right now…

(under nose) I feel grateful for my abundance…

(chin) I am happy now anyway…

(collarbone) I love feeling good…

(under arm) I am wealthy in spirit no matter what…

(head) I feel grateful for my abundance.

ISSUE: BELIEF IN POVERTY

If you have a philosophical "belief" in poverty, the energetic resonance of this belief could be a self-fulfilling prophecy. Say the statement out loud, and measure *how true* it feels to you on the 0-10 point **Intensity Scale**.

- *I'm convinced I will always be poor* _____ (0-10)

*(Repeat the following **setup statement** 3 times while tapping the **karate chop point**.)*

> *Even though **I'm convinced I will always be poor**, that's just who I am, I deeply and completely accept all of me.*

ROUND #1: Negative Reminder Phrase

*(Repeat the following **reminder phrase** while tapping the sequence of 8 tapping points.)*

> *I'm convinced I will always be poor.*

How does this conviction feel to you now that you have tapped on it? Is the "truth" of it still as high? Continue tapping until the conviction feels much weaker, and then continue with the positive phrases below.

ROUND #2: Positive Phrases

(Repeat a different phrase for each of the 8 tapping points.)

(eyebrow) I am wealthy already...

(side of eye) I love feeling the abundance in my life...

(under eye) There is plenty of abundance already...

(under nose) I love feeling free about success...

(chin) I am wealthy already...

(collarbone) I feel abundance in my life...

(under arm) There is plenty of abundance everywhere...

(head) I love feeling free about success.

ISSUE: I COME FROM A FAMILY OF FAILURES

This may be 100% factually true, but it has nothing to do with your ability to succeed in whatever you put your mind to today. There may be generations of failures on both sides of your family, but what does it have to do with you?

Measure the "truth" of these statements on the 0-10 point scale:

- *I'm convinced I'll fail like my parents* _____ (0-10)
- *I'm just like him in every way, so I'll fail too* _____ (0-10)
- *If I come from a family of failures, it is inevitable that I will fail too* _____ (0-10)

If any of these above statements measured higher than a 3 on the 0-10 point **Intensity Scale**, you have some serious tapping to do on this limiting belief! Again, I'm not arguing that your ancestors were failures or not, *I'm just reminding you that it has nothing to do with your ability to succeed.*

*(Repeat the following **setup statements** while tapping the **karate chop point**.)*

*Even though **I'm convinced I have to be a failure** just like my parents and grandparents, I deeply and completely love and accept myself anyway...Even though **I'm certain I'll be a failure too**, I accept who I am and how I feel...Even though **I'm using them as my excuse to fail**, I deeply and completely love and accept myself.*

ROUND #1: Negative Reminder Phrase

*(Repeat the following **reminder phrase** while tapping the sequence of 8 tapping points.)*

I'm convinced I have to fail like other family members.

ROUND #2: Positive Phrases

(Repeat a different phrase for each of the 8 tapping points.)

(eyebrow) I choose to be different and still love them…

(side of eye) I don't have to be a failure just because they were…

(under eye) I choose to move forward with my life…

(under nose) I deserve success even if they didn't believe they did…

(chin) I choose to be a success no matter what…

(collarbone) I am a success already…

(under arm) I choose success instead of failure…

(head) I feel fantastic about all my successes already.

Measure the belief/conviction about being a failure because of your ancestry…and continue tapping until it has been significantly reduced and you feel confident that you will be a success regardless of your parents' and grandparents' failures.

ISSUE: YES, BUT…

*(Repeat the following **setup statement** 3 times while tapping the **karate chop point**.)*

*Even though **I'm not rich yet**, I choose to expect abundance in my life.*

ROUND #1: Negative Reminder Phrase

*(Repeat the following **reminder phrase** while tapping the sequence of 8 tapping points.)*

I'm not rich yet.

ROUND #2: Positive Phrases

(Repeat a different phrase for each of the 8 tapping points.)

(eyebrow) I love feeling wealthy…

(side of eye) I choose to feel rich…

(under eye) I love feeling abundance all around me…

(under nose) I choose success now…

(chin) I am already feeling wealthy…

(collarbone) I choose to feel rich…

(under arm) I love feeling abundance all around me…

(head) I choose success now.

KEEP TAPPING...IT WORKS

Here are some additional questions to help uncover the reasons you may be *attracting the opposite* of what you want in your life:

- **Are you constantly complaining about *how few good men* (or women) there are in your town?**

Many of my clients blame New York City for their uninspired love lives. New York is not the source of their problem. The *attitude of scarcity*, (*there aren't enough single men/women*) is the source of the problem.

How satisfied are you with your *love life?* Are you constantly thinking there aren't enough potential partners in your town? Try thinking thoughts of *abundance* and *vibrating* in a new way to *attract your mate* into your life.

164

- **Are you focused on the ailments typically found within your age group?**

Remember that your focus on ailments will bring them right into your life. Wouldn't you rather focus on how strong certain parts of your body feel, and how well your body has supported you?

- **Have you always been *desperate* to lose weight?**

People who feel desperate about losing weight are chronically focused on the parts of their body they want to get rid of…which means those parts can in fact grow right before their very eyes! Use **EFT** to alleviate the focus on fat and the negative tone of your vibration. You will never see food as the enemy again. Remember, *you can't get thin when you feel fat!* This next section will address issues of love, health, and body weight.

ISSUE: IT'S NORMAL TO COMPLAIN AND SUFFER

Maybe it is typical, common and habitual to complain and suffer, but that doesn't mean you have to fall into this category. You don't have to complain and suffer, it's a choice of focus.

I admit and agree that bad habits are hard to change. The urge and pull back towards these bad habits is indeed seductive, and as I've said earlier, knowing what to expect of yourself and your habits is worth a lot.

> **Suppose it is "normal" in our particular society to complain and suffer...**
> **How "normal" do you want to be?**

Keep tapping on this issue until you no longer want or feel compelled to complain and suffer, even if it still seems typical for your social group.

(Repeat the following **setup statements** *while tapping the* **karate chop point.***)*

> *Even though* **it's normal to complain and suffer***, I choose to accept who I am and how I feel...Even though* **I've been complaining and suffering for so long I wouldn't know how to do something else***, I deeply and completely love and accept myself anyway...Even though* **I'm not sure I want to change this habit***, I accept who I am and how I feel.*

ROUND #1: Negative Reminder Phrase

*(Repeat the following **reminder phrase** while tapping the sequence of 8 tapping points.)*

It's normal to complain and suffer.

ROUND #2: Positive Phrases

(Repeat a different phrase for each of the 8 tapping points.)

(eyebrow) I choose to change this habit…

(side of eye) I feel excited to change this habit…

(under eye) I choose joy in my life…

(under nose) I deserve to feel happy no matter what...

(chin) I choose joy instead of suffering…

(collarbone) I appreciate who I am and how I feel...

(under arm) I choose joyful thoughts and feelings…

(head) I appreciate who I am and who I'm becoming.

ISSUE: ATTRACTING ROMANTIC PARTNER

*(Repeat the following **setup statements** while tapping the **karate chop point**.)*

*Even though **I can't seem to find the right mate**, I deeply and completely accept myself anyway...Even though **I'm convinced I'll always be single**, I choose to accept who I am and how I feel...Even though **I feel jealous because they have mates and I don't**, I accept how I feel.*

ROUND #1: Negative Reminder Phrase

*(Repeat the following **reminder phrase** while tapping the sequence of 8 tapping points.)*

I can't seem to find the right mate.

ROUND #2: Positive Phrases

(Repeat a different phrase for each of the 8 tapping points.)

(eyebrow) Many people have been successful in this area...

(side of eye) I love knowing my mate is on his/her way...

(under eye) I know I will be ready when he/she appears...

(under nose) The Universe is bringing me what I want...

(chin) Many people have been successful in this area...

(collarbone) My mate is on his/her way to me...

(under arm) I will be so ready when he/she appears...

(head) I appreciate attracting my mate.

ISSUE: FEAR OF REJECTION

*(Repeat the following **setup statements** while tapping the **karate chop point**.)*

*Even though **I'm afraid they will reject me**, I deeply and completely accept myself...Even though **I don't feel worthy of a faithful mate**, I choose to feel worthy now...Even though **I don't feel lovable, and never have**, I choose to feel good now.*

ROUND #1: Negative Reminder Phrase

*(Repeat the following **reminder phrase** while tapping the sequence of 8 tapping points.)*

I don't feel worthy of a faithful mate.

ROUND #2: Positive Phrases

(Repeat a different phrase for each of the 8 tapping points.)

(eyebrow) I love feeling accepted...

(side of eye) I remember feeling accepted...

(under eye) I choose to feel lovable...

(under nose) I know I am lovable now...

(chin) I feel worthy...

(collarbone) I am acceptable...

(under arm) I choose to feel lovable...

(head) I know I am lovable now.

ISSUE: FOCUS ON AGING

If you fear aging, it's a *tappable* issue as all fears are! Say the statement below out loud and measure how high your fear is about the topic. Remember, the fear and focus on aging will bring energetic attention to it.

- *I'm afraid of aging* _____ (0-10)

(Repeat the following **setup statements** *while tapping the* **karate chop point.***)*

> *Even though* **I feel pain when I walk**, *I deeply and completely accept myself...Even though* **I'm afraid of aging**, *I choose to feel energy flowing through my body...Even though* **I'm afraid my body is failing**, *I choose to feel energetic today.*

ROUND #1: Negative Reminder Phrase

(Repeat the following **reminder phrase** *while tapping the sequence of 8 tapping points.)*

> *I'm afraid of aging.*

Hopefully, your fear has been reduced by tapping on it. Did you find any additional thoughts and feelings that were also *tappable* issues? Devise your own *Setup Statements* and continue tapping.

ROUND #2: Positive Phrases

(Repeat a different phrase for each of the 8 tapping points.)

(eyebrow) I love feeling energetic...

(side of eye) I love my healthy body...

(under eye) I feel so happy about the strength of my body...

(under nose) I believe in my body's ability to heal itself...

(chin) I love feeling energetic...

(collarbone) I love feeling strong...

(under arm) I feel so happy about the strength of my body...

(head)   I feel so healthy and strong.

ISSUE: FEELING FAT

Measure *how true* these statements feel to you, and how intense your emotions are about them:

- *I feel fat* _____ (0-10)

- *I feel hopeless about losing weight* _____ (0-10)

- *I'll always be fat* _____ (0-10)

*(Repeat the following **setup statement** 3 times while tapping the **karate chop point**.)*

Even though ***I feel fat and hopeless about losing weight**, I deeply and completely accept myself anyway.*

ROUND #1: Negative Reminder Phrase

*(Repeat the following **reminder phrase** while tapping the sequence of 8 tapping points.)*

I feel fat and hopeless about losing weight.

Measure the statements again…***how true*** do they feel now and how high is the emotion on them?

- *I feel fat* _____ (0-10)

- *I feel hopeless about losing weight* _____ (0-10)

- *I'll always be fat* _____ (0-10)

ROUND #2: Positive Phrases

(Repeat a different phrase for each of the 8 tapping points.)

(eyebrow) I love feeling thin...

(side of eye) I could feel thin...

(under eye) I'm allowed to feel thin...

(under nose) I want to feel thin...

(chin) I choose to feel thin...

(collarbone) I allow myself to feel slender...

(under arm) I allow myself to feel good about my body...

(head) I appreciate my body now.

ABUNDANCE GAMES

END RESULT IMAGERY

END RESULT IMAGERY is used by athletes, sales people and anyone interested in reaching their goals quickly. Again, it is a kind of *recipe*. Use all the ingredients to speed up the delivery of your goal.

See yourself having accomplished your goal.

Hear two supportive friends congratulating you on achieving what you wanted.

Feel the emotions of your success.

Sense how your body feels now that you have reached your goal.

Smell whatever aromas might be connected to this success. (A client of mine said she would buy expensive perfume if she reached her goal.)

Taste what success tastes like to you.

Combine all these images and sensations together again and visualize yourself having attained your goal.

TAKE FIVE

Imagery needs to be very clear and sharp. It also needs to be believable. Whenever I use this next exercise that I call **TAKE FIVE** and follow it with a *Statement of Thanks and Gratitude*, my *vibration* improves immediately and dramatically. I still find it hard to write out this exercise without grinning ear to ear! Try it if you are serious about *receiving* what you want. Here are the basic ingredients of this *recipe*. You will be writing out your statements in this order:

- *KNOW* what you want
- *STATE YOUR INTENTION*
- *CHOOSE* to see yourself with your goal
- *BELIEVE* and *EXPECT* your success
- *ACT AS IF* you already have what you want
- *GIVE THANKS* for achieving the end result

Start by *identifying specifically* what you want to *attract* in your life and write it out on paper. Play around with the words so your statement is succinct and really communicates *exactly* what you are looking for. You may choose tangible material items such as a car, home or jewelry, or "intangibles" such as spiritual fulfillment, a higher vibration, or a feeling of peace. For example, you may want:

(1) a new BMW sports car/ or a new home

(2) a higher vibration around money ($$)

(3) the perfect business partner

(4) $2 million dollars through surprising channels

(5) the perfect life partner

Follow the examples below for your **5 statements**. Then write out a *Statement of Thanks and Gratitude*.

- *I WANT* to attract a higher vibration about money.

- *I INTEND* to attract a higher vibration about money.

- *I CHOOSE* to attract a higher vibration about money.

- *I EXPECT* to attract a higher vibration about money.

- *I AM ALREADY ATTRACTING* a higher vibration about money.

THANK YOU UNIVERSE (God, Spirit, Higher Power) *for allowing me to attract a higher vibration about money!*

- *I WANT* to attract the ideal home for me.

- *I INTEND* to attract the ideal home for me.

- *I CHOOSE* to attract the ideal home for me.

- *I EXPECT* to attract the ideal home for me.

- *I AM ALREADY ATTRACTING* the ideal home for me.

THANK YOU UNIVERSE (God, Spirit, Higher Power) *for bringing me the ideal home.*

STEP #4

CLAIM

ABUNDANCE

NOW

STEP #4
CLAIM ABUNDANCE NOW

Many people are afraid to own or *claim the abundance* that is waiting for them. They suddenly feel shy when offered an amazing opportunity, or don't know how to "close the deal." *Abundance* is available to all of us, but we must activate our positive intentions to *claim success* or it will slip away.

- **Do you have trouble *believing you can have* what you want?**

Frederick didn't believe he could have what he had always dreamed about, so he could never *claim abundance*, assuming it wasn't *his* to have. With some easy tapping suggestions, he broke down the belief system that fueled this assumption: his father had told him he would never get what he wanted and that he *should settle* for whatever he could get.

If you don't *believe* you deserve to have what you want, stop trying to *get what you want* until you address the underlying belief system with **EFT** and positive affirmations. Otherwise, all your efforts will be a waste of time.

- **Do you still feel that you *don't deserve abundance* or wealth?**

While we touched upon *deserving issues* under **STEP 2**, there is always more to clear with this topic. Many people suffer from the overall belief *"I don't deserve success."*

This ***belief***, or conviction, naturally undermines success. My client Jonathon never felt deserving of wealth. Because of his intelligence, he always did well and never had to work very hard. He found this an unfair advantage, and as a result, didn't think he deserved wealth as much as others who worked overtime. Until Jonathon dealt with this basic belief system, none of his self-help books or hours of counseling with a top coach in the country moved him towards his goals.

ISSUE: SELF-WORTH

If you still don't believe that you deserve success, look into the reasons why this may be true.

- ### *I don't deserve success* _____ (0-10)

    o Why don't you feel deserving of success?
    o Who taught you this?
    o Do others deserve success?
    o What is this based on?

*(Repeat the following **setup statements** while tapping the **karate chop point**.)*

> *Even though **I don't believe I deserve success**, I completely accept who I am...Even though **I'm convinced others deserve and I don't**, I choose to believe in my worthiness now...Even though **I don't believe I can have what I want**, I choose to change my beliefs around money.*

ROUND #1: Negative Reminder Phrase

*(Repeat the following **reminder phrase** while tapping the sequence of 8 tapping points.)*

> ### *I don't believe I deserve success.*

ROUND #2: Positive Phrases

(Repeat a different phrase for each of the 8 tapping points.)

(eyebrow) I believe I deserve money...

(side of eye) I know I deserve success and abundance...

(under eye) I appreciate abundance everywhere...

(under nose) I love appreciating abundance in my life...

(chin) I believe I deserve money...

(collarbone) I know I deserve prosperity...

(under arm) I appreciate abundance in the lives of others...

(head) I love appreciating abundance in my life.

ISSUE: I'M NOT WORTHY

*(Repeat the following **setup statements** while tapping the **karate chop point**.)*

*Even though **they told me I didn't deserve any more**, I choose to believe differently now...Even though **they convinced me I wasn't worthy**, I choose to believe in my worth now...Even though **I have always felt unworthy**, I choose to feel valuable now.*

ROUND #1: Negative Reminder Phrase

*(Repeat the following **reminder phrase** while tapping the sequence of 8 tapping points.)*

They convinced me I wasn't worthy.

ROUND #2: Positive Phrases

(Repeat a different phrase for each of the 8 tapping points.)

(eyebrow) I believe in my worth...

(side of eye) I am enough...

(under eye) There is enough for everyone...

(under nose) I love believing I am worthy now...

(chin) I believe in my worth...

(collarbone) I am profoundly lovable...

(under arm) There is enough for everyone...

(head) I love believing I am worthy now.

ISSUE: SUCCESS IS NOT FOR ME

*(Repeat the following **setup statements** while tapping the **karate chop point**.)*

*Even though **I'm still convinced I'm not worthy of success**, I deeply and completely love and accept all of me...Even though **I'm convinced success is not meant for me**, I choose to claim abundance now...Even though **I'm not someone who should be abundant**, I choose to believe in myself.*

ROUND #1: Negative Reminder Phrase

*(Repeat the following **reminder phrase** while tapping the sequence of 8 tapping points.)*

I'm still convinced I'm not worthy of success.

ROUND #2: Positive Phrases

(Repeat a different phrase for each of the 8 tapping points.)

(eyebrow) I am worthy…

(side of eye) No I'm not…

(under eye) Yes I am…

(under nose) I am worthy of abundance and so are you…

(chin) I am worthy now…

(collarbone) I'm glad the conflict is over…

(under arm) Yes I am worthy now and always have been…

(head) I am worthy of abundance and so are you.

ISSUE: I DON'T DESERVE ABUNDANCE

*(Repeat the following **setup statements** while tapping the **karate chop point**.)*

*Even though **I have trouble accepting abundance**, I choose to claim it now...Even though **I don't feel right having financial worth**, I deeply and completely accept myself anyway...Even though **I still don't feel deserving of happiness**, I choose to change this pattern.*

ROUND #1: Negative Reminder Phrase

*(Repeat the following **reminder phrase** while tapping the sequence of 8 tapping points.)*

I still don't feel deserving of abundance.

ROUND #2: Positive Phrases

(Repeat a different phrase for each of the 8 tapping points.)

(eyebrow) I choose to accept abundance starting now...

(side of eye) We are all allowed to accept abundance...

(under eye) I choose to feel worthy of all that I want...

(under nose) I deserve happiness...I know it is coming...

(chin) I choose to accept abundance starting now...

(collarbone) We are all allowed to claim abundance...

(under arm) I choose to feel worthy of all that I want...

(head) I feel deserving of happiness and know it is coming to me.

ISSUE: I SHOULDN'T CLAIM SUCCESS

*(Repeat the following **setup statements** while tapping the **karate chop point**.)*

---

*Even though **I continue to sabotage myself**, I choose to release this pattern...Even though **I don't feel clear about what I want**, I choose to accept the clarity now...Even though **I still don't feel I deserve success**, I choose to believe that I do now.*

ROUND #1: Negative Reminder Phrase

*(Repeat the following **reminder phrase** while tapping the sequence of 8 tapping points.)*

I continue to sabotage myself.

ROUND #2: Positive Phrases

(Repeat a different phrase for each of the 8 tapping points.)

(eyebrow) I love feeling clear about my success…

(side of eye) I choose to feel clear about my goals…

(under eye) I love knowing I am reaching my goals…

(under nose) I appreciate all the abundance in my life…

(chin) I love claiming my success…

(collarbone) I choose to feel clarity in my life…

(under arm) I love knowing I am reaching my goals…

(head) I appreciate all the abundance in my life.

ISSUE: SUCCESS ISN'T "SPIRITUAL"

*(Repeat the following **setup statements** while tapping the **karate chop point**.)*

*Even though **I don't think wanting wealth is spiritual,** I choose to release this false belief...Even though **I'm afraid they won't see me as spiritual**, I choose to remain connected to my Source...Even though **I'm afraid being prosperous isn't spiritual**, I choose to know how deeply spiritual I am.*

ROUND #1: Negative Reminder Phrase

*(Repeat the following **reminder phrase** while tapping the sequence of 8 tapping points.)*

I'm afraid success isn't "spiritual."

ROUND #2: Positive Phrases

(Repeat a different phrase for each of the 8 tapping points.)

(eyebrow) I'm afraid being wealthy isn't spiritual...

(side of eye) I remember how spiritual I am...

(under eye) I love knowing how much integrity I have...

(under nose) I know my values are solid...

(chin) I love remembering my spiritual values...

(collarbone) I choose to feel clear about my spiritual goals...

(under arm) I love knowing I am deeply connected...

(head) I appreciate all the spiritual abundance in my life.

ISSUE: FEELING LACK

*(Repeat the following **setup statements** while tapping the **karate chop point**.)*

*Even though **I still feel lack in my life**, I choose to feel plenty now...Even though **I still think there won't be enough for me**, I love feeling plenty now...Even though **I'm afraid to claim my abundance**...I choose to claim it now!*

ROUND #1: Negative Reminder Phrase

*(Repeat the following **reminder phrase** while tapping the sequence of 8 tapping points.)*

I'm afraid to claim my abundance.

ROUND #2: Positive Phrases

(Repeat a different phrase for each of the 8 tapping points.)

(eyebrow) I claim abundance now…

(side of eye) I choose to feel all the abundance in my life…

(under eye) I am receiving success every day…

(under nose) I am grateful for all the blessings I have…

(chin) I claim abundance now…

(collarbone) I feel so much prosperity…

(under arm) I am receiving success every day…

(head) I am grateful for all the blessings in my life.

ISSUE: LIFE HAS TO BE A STRUGGLE

*(Repeat the following **setup statements** while tapping the **karate chop point**.)*

*Even though **I'm convinced life has to be a struggle**, I choose to feel easy about it now...Even **though I don't know what it feels like to relax about money**, I choose to believe it can be easy...Even though **I don't know how to stop the struggle**, I choose to relax now!*

ROUND #1: Negative Reminder Phrase

*(Repeat the following **reminder phrase** while tapping the sequence of 8 tapping points.)*

I'm convinced life has to be a struggle.

ROUND #2: Positive Phrases

(Repeat a different phrase for each of the 8 tapping points.)

(eyebrow) Isn't life supposed to be difficult?

(side of eye) What if it's supposed to be easy?

(under eye) What if it could be easy?

(under nose) I appreciate knowing there is a new way...

(chin) I love knowing I can do it differently...

(collarbone) I love that money comes easily to me now...

(under arm) I'm grateful for how relaxed I feel...

(head) I appreciate all the blessings in my life.

ISSUE: I'M AFRAID OF MY POWER

Many of my clients have caught a glimpse of their emotional power, integrity and ability to get what they want when they focus on being in full alignment with their desires. When they practice feeling and exuding vibrations that match their goals, out pops a desired gift from the Universe. This can feel a little spooky, and certainly too good to be true. *But it IS good, and it IS true.*

Numerous clients tell me that when they figured out how to use the *Law of Attraction* for their own good, the "recipe" seemed so easy that it felt like they were cheating! More importantly, they felt scared of their power when they were in alignment.

When people realize how full, rich and passionate their life could be, something about it feels overwhelming, even threatening. Many workshop attendees have told me that deep down they are afraid of how successful, happy and congruent they could be if they kept in vibrational alignment with their desires.

Measure the "truth" of the following statements on the 0-10 point **Intensity Scale**:

- *I'm afraid of my power* _____ (0-10)

- *I'm afraid of what they'll think of my power* _____ (0-10)

- *I'm afraid of feeling too powerful _____ (0-10)*

*(Repeat the following **setup statements** while tapping the **karate chop point**.)*

> *Even though **I'm afraid of my own power**, I deeply and profoundly love and accept myself anyway...Even though **I'm afraid of how powerful I really am**, I choose to feel calm and confident anyway...Even though **I'm afraid of my power**, I deeply and completely love and accept myself anyway.*

ROUND #1: Negative Reminder Phrase

*(Repeat the following **reminder phrase** while tapping the sequence of 8 tapping points.)*

> *I'm afraid of my power.*

How does this feel to you now? Are you still afraid of your power? Do you understand where this fear came from in your life?

- *I'm still afraid of my power _____ (0-10)*

Continue tapping on this fear of your emotional/energetic power, and then move on to the positive phrases below.

ROUND #2: Positive Phrases

(Repeat a different phrase for each of the 8 tapping points.)

(eyebrow) I choose to accept my power...

(side of eye) We are all powerful...

(under eye) I choose to embrace my power...

(under nose) I deserve to be powerful like everyone else...

(chin) I embrace and appreciate my power...

(collarbone) I enjoy feeling powerful instead of helpless...

(under arm) I choose to accept all of my power now...

(head) I feel confident, calm and powerful now.

Continue tapping rounds on your fear of being powerful until it no longer bothers you or no longer registers on the 0-10 point **Intensity Scale**.

POSITIVE

AFFIRMATIONS

POSITIVE AFFIRMATIONS

Lack of clarity resulting from inner emotional static definitely blocks *attracting abundance*. Insert whatever word you prefer for "Spirit" or "God" as you say the following phrases *while tapping*:

- *I choose to feel connected to my SOURCE*

- *I love feeling connected to Spirit*

- *I love hearing divine guidance from Spirit*

- *I love feeling clarity about receiving guidance*

- *I love appreciating all of God's messages*

- *I hear, see and feel the next right step*

For basic *positive affirmations*, to use throughout the day but not necessarily while you are tapping, try the following:

- *I am enough, there is enough*

- *I claim success now; I am successful now*

- *I am grateful for all the abundance in my life*

- *Thank you for all the blessings I have*

- *I love prosperity, I receive guidance*

- *I rejoice in all of our prosperity*

- *I am grateful that SPIRIT knows we are all worthy*

ABUNDANCE GAMES

THE YES GAME

I find the positive energy of the **YES GAME** very contagious. Try this: Write a list of questions to which the answer is definitely, undeniably, *YES.*

Write the questions out on a piece of paper and ask a friend to read the list to you. Make sure your friend pauses for your answer each time, or read the list out loud to yourself and enthusiastically respond *YES!* to each question. If at any time your response seems lukewarm, that means you need to tweak the question so that it is easier to be joyful about the *YES* answer. Start the list with obvious questions:

- **Is your name Carol Look?** *YES!*
- **Do you live in New York?** *YES!*
- **Do you want to attract $5 million dollars?** *YES!*
- **Do you love your home?** *YES!*
- **Do you believe in the work you do?** *YES!*
- **Are your favorite colors blue and purple?** *YES!*
- **Don't you just love puppies and kittens?** *YES!*

Then move to more important questions…

- **Do you know you are *successful* already? *YES!***
- **Does the *Law of Attraction* work? *YES!***
- **Do you *appreciate* your clients? *YES!***
- **Are you *happy* with the flow of your life? *YES!***
- **Do you *appreciate* that money comes easily? *YES!***

Your list of **questions** may cover any topics you wish. Just make sure you can answer them with an emphatic *YES!*

THE THANK YOU GAME

The **THANK YOU GAME** is very simple and uses *statements of gratitude* in the present tense to *Thank the Universe* for what you want to *attract* in to your life. Remember, what you *put out* to the *Universe* will be returned to you like a boomerang. (Imagine hearing an echo coming back to you.) Start tapping at your *eyebrow point* and follow 2 or 3 rounds in a row:

- *Thank you Universe for my abundance.*

- *Thank you Universe for my vibrant health.*

- *Thank you Universe for such rich friendships.*

- *Thank you Universe for financial success.*

- *Thank you Universe for exciting opportunities.*

- *Thank you Universe for all the blessings in my life.*

Also, you may use these phrases without tapping, and repeat them while you clean the house or walk your dog.

- *Thank you Universe for my insight about my health.*

- *Thank you Universe for bringing me financial abundance.*

- *Thank you Universe for showing me the next right step.*

- *Thank you Universe for all my loving friends.*

- *Thank you Universe for bringing me such clarity.*

WHAT NEXT? WHAT NEXT? WHAT NEXT?

Now you have dozens of **EFT statements**, *positive affirmations*, *visualization techniques*, *written exercises*, and *abundance games* to use to break through your comfort zones and limiting beliefs. You have enough *RECIPES* for hundreds of gourmet meals!

NOW ALL YOU HAVE TO DO IS USE THEM

I make time every day to use **EFT**, meditate, write, or play one or more of the *Abundance Games* outlined in this book. This commitment has paid off immensely and I continue to put aside and cherish this time for myself.

Using **EFT**, you will be able to *attract the success and abundance* that you are entitled to in this lifetime. I encourage you to confidently communicate your worth to the *universe* and...

CLAIM

YOUR

ABUNDANCE

RIGHT NOW!

TROUBLESHOOTING PLAN

How do you feel now? Is your overall abundance picture looking brighter to you? If not, below is a *trouble-shooting plan* for you. I highly recommend you examine each point and work on whatever steps are necessary in order to speed up your success. Below is my 10 point plan to rejuvenate your life of abundance.

1. How Much Tapping Are You Doing?

Are you putting aside time every day to do your tapping to clear your abundance issues? *Attracting Abundance* isn't exactly magic, you do need to do your tapping!

2. How Specific Are You in Your EFT Rounds?

If you don't seem to be making much progress, you may need to tweak the language in your rounds of **EFT** to become more specific. In other words, instead of saying "these blocks to abundance" you might specify which block… *"this fear of being someone different."*

3. Are You Actually Playing the *Abundance Games*?

The **Abundance Games** listed in this book are critical to your success. Some of them seem so simple, it may be hard to remember to write or play them every day. Put the games back on your daily "have fun" list.

4. Are You Drinking Enough Water?

Some practitioners believe that dehydration can block progress with **EFT**. Considering that we are addressing the electricity in our bodies through the ancient Chinese meridian network of energetic pathways, and water conducts electricity, I recommend upping your water intake for general health purposes...and if it helps with any **EFT** blocks, great.

5. Being Doctor and Patient at the Same Time:

It can certainly be a challenge to play the role of doctor and patient at the same time. We all have blind spots about our own issues, so if you feel stuck at all, it may be a good time to contact an **EFT** practitioner for objectivity and wisdom.

6. Hidden Issues:

What issues are you actually hiding from yourself? You know, those issues you don't want to admit out loud...these issues need attention and tapping!

7. Daily Attitude of Gratitude:

If you are having difficulty writing out your gratitude list every day, change the focus to a list of (1) 10 things I feel happy about today, or (2) 10 things that make me feel relief.

8. Forgiveness:

Go back over the list of childhood events that may have contributed to your blocks to receiving of abundance. What family members, coaches or teachers do you need to forgive?

9. Remaining Blocks:

If there were topics or relationships I didn't cover in this book, feel free to devise all your own **EFT Setup Statements** and continue tapping on any remaining blocks you have to attracting success and abundance.

10. Delete Your Impatience...

Since I am one of the most impatient people I know, I am well aware that being impatient about attracting abundance does nothing but delay what I want! I invite you to tap on impatience, enjoy what you DO have, and feel excited about what's coming down the road for you.

It is coming... and sooner than you expect.

ADDITIONAL EFT TRAINING

To boost your success and abundance, the following **EFT** training products are offered through **www.AttractingAbundance.com**:

- **Audio CDs:** *The Vibration of Abundance*

- **Audio CDs:** *Business Abundance Now*

- **Audio CDs:** *Weight Loss with EFT*

- **Audio CDs:** *Healing the Cycle of Addiction*

- **Downloadable mp3 Files:** *Clearing Clutter with EFT*

- **Downloadable mp3 Files:** *Eliminating Your Fear of Public Speaking*

- **Training Manual:** *Quit Smoking Now*

- **Paperback and e-book:** *It's Not About the Food*

- **Paperback and e-book:** *Improve Your Eyesight with EFT*

- **DVDs:** *Success and Abundance with EFT and the Law of Attraction*

- **DVDs:** *A Vibrational Approach to Healing Pain and Illness*

- **DVDs:** *The EFT and Law of Attraction* **Atlanta Workshop led by "The Secret" expert Bob Doyle and EFT Master Carol Look** **www.wealthbeyondreason.com/atlantadvd.html**

- **Membership Audio & Coaching Program: www.PainReliefwithEFT.com**

- **Electronic EFT:** *The Key to Weight Loss*

ESSENTIAL WEB SITES

www.AttractingAbundance.com

www.TapTalkRadio.com

www.PainReliefwithEFT.com

www.TheTappingSolution.com

www.Abraham-Hicks.com

Special thanks to EFT Founder Gary Craig for his generosity, support, and tireless efforts to spread the word about EFT around the world.

Special thanks to EFT Coach and Pain Relief Specialist Rick Wilkes of www.Thrivingnow.com for exceptional technical and editorial support with this project.

RECOMMENDED READING

1. Dahl, Linda Madden. *Ten Thousand Whispers: A Guide to Conscious Creation*. Eugene, OR: The Woodbridge Group. 1995.

2. Demartini, John F. *Count Your Blessings: The Healing Power of Gratitude and Love*. Rockport, MA: Element Books, Inc. 1997.

3. Dooley, Mike. *Notes From the Universe: New Perspectives From An Old Friend*. Orlando, FL: TUT Enterprises, Inc. 2003.

4. Doyle, Bob. *Wealth Beyond Reason*. Canada: www.Trafford.com. 2003.

5. Dyer, Dr. Wayne D. *The Power of Intention: Learning to Co-create Your World Your Way*. Carlsbad, CA: Hay House, Inc. 2004.

6. Grabhorn, Lynn. *Excuse Me, Your Life is Waiting*. Charlottesville, VA: Hampton Roads Publishing Company, Inc. 2000.

7. Hicks, Jerry and Esther. *The Law of Attraction: The Basics of the Teachings of Abraham*. Carlsbad, CA: Hay House, Inc. 2006.

8. Holmes, Ernest. *The Science of Mind: A Philosophy, A Faith, A Way of Life.* New York, NY: Jeremy P. Tarcher/Putnam. 1938.

9. Kehoe, John. *Mind Power.* British Columbia, Canada: Zoetic Inc. 1997.

10. Loveland-Coen, Victoria. *Manifesting Your Desires.* Sherman Oaks, CA: Self-Mastery Press. 1998.

11. Murphy, Joseph. *Think Yourself Rich.* Paramus, NJ: Reward Books. 2001.

12. Ponder, Catherine. *Secret of Unlimited Prosperity.* Marina del Ray, CA: DeVorss Publications. 1981.

13. Price, John Randolph. *The Abundance Book.* Carlsbad, CA: Hay House, Inc. 1987.

14. Roberts, Jane. *The Nature of Personal Reality.* San Rafael, CA: Amber-Allen Publishing. 1994.

ABOUT THE AUTHOR

EFT Master Carol Look is an author, international workshop leader and former internet radio show host. Known for being a leading voice in the Energy Psychology community and bringing innovations to **EFT**, Carol's specialty is inspiring clients to *attract abundance* into their lives by using **EFT** to clear limiting beliefs, release resistance and build their "prosperity consciousness."

Before becoming trained in numerous *Energy Psychology* methods, Carol was trained as a **Clinical Social Worker** and earned her Doctoral Degree in **Clinical Hypnotherapy**. She was among the first group of practitioners in the world to be certified by **Emotional Freedom Techniques (EFT)** founder Gary Craig as an **EFT Master**.

Carol's books, *Attracting Abundance with EFT* and *Improve Your Eyesight with EFT*, are also available as e-books with companion audio recordings. Carol is the author of two of the field's classic **EFT** training manuals, *How to Lose Weight with Energy Therapy* (soon to be republished under the new title: *It's Not About the Food*) and *Quit Smoking Now with Energy Therapy*.

She also sells a variety of audio CD programs on the following topics: ***Business Abundance Now, The Vibration of Abundance, Weight Loss with Energy Therapy***, and ***Healing the Cycle of Addiction***. Carol has collaborated with colleagues to create numerous downloadable mp3 programs such as ***Clearing Clutter with EFT*** and ***Eliminating Your Fear of Public Speaking***, and launched the field's first Pain Relief membership audio and coaching program, ***Pain Relief with EFT***, with energy practitioner and pain specialist, Rick Wilkes. Her DVD training sets include ***Success and Abundance with EFT and the Law of Attraction*** and ***A Vibrational Approach to Healing Pain and Illness.***

The focus of Carol's clinical work is leading **EFT** workshops worldwide on the topics of *Attracting Abundance, Pain Relief, Clearing Addictions*, and *Weight Loss.* She has taught **EFT** classes for organizations such as the *National Guild of Hypnotists* **(NGH)**, the *Association of Comprehensive Energy Psychology* **(ACEP)**, the *National Institute for the Clinical Application of Behavioral Medicine* **(NICABM)**, the *Toronto Energy Psychology Conference* (**Toronto-EPC**), the *Psychotherapy Networker Symposium*, and the *Center for Spirituality and Psychotherapy* (**CSP**).